Work
and Career

CHOICES

GUIDES FOR TODAY'S WOMAN

Work
and Career

Nancy van Vuuren

The Westminster Press
Philadelphia

Scripture quotations from the Revised Standard Version of the Bible are copyrighted 1946, 1952, © 1971, 1973 by the Division of Christian Education of the National Council of the Churches of Christ in the U.S.A., and are used by permission.

Book Design by Alice Derr

First edition

Published by The Westminster Press®
Philadelphia, Pennsylvania .

PRINTED IN THE UNITED STATES OF AMERICA

9 8 7 6 5 4 3 2 1

Library of Congress Cataloging in Publication Data

Van Vuuren, Nancy, 1938–
Work and Career

  (Choices : guides for today's woman)
  1. Vocation. 2. Vocational guidance for women.
3. Women—Employment. I. Title. II. Title: Work and career. III. Series.
BV4740.V36 1983   248.8'43   83-12338
ISBN 0-664-24539-0 (pbk.)

CONTENTS

PUBLISHER'S ACKNOWLEDGMENT

The publisher gratefully acknowledges the advice of several distinguished scholars in planning this series. Virginia Mollenkott, Arlene Swidler, Phyllis Trible, and Ann Ulanov helped shape the goals of the series, identify vital topics, and locate knowledgeable authors. Views expressed in the books, of course, are those of the individual writers and not of the advisers.

PROLOGUE

A woman must take her lifework seriously, as part of her being and of her belief. This book is intended to help you to realize and to choose actively from the options available to you. The choices, the decisions, must ultimately be made in faith, through prayer and meditation, by listening.

To choose, to make decisions, though, a woman must know, love, and respect herself. She must be knowledgeable about the world in which she is functioning and choosing: marriage, raising children, volunteering her time and skills, working for pay, surviving.

Although this book may provide some of the information needed, it is intended more to help you ask the questions necessary to meaningful life-planning and life decisions. For the church this book can serve as the tool in organizing and holding life-planning seminars involving women of various age groups, and in establishing support groups among women in the parish and the community.

CHAPTER 1

What Is Work?

Work is a word that has almost as many different meanings as there are people who use the word. That is the reason careful thinking about work is so important, particularly to women.

Usually the word "work" is used to mean being hired by someone and paid money to do a specific task at a specific time and place—being employed. The money earned is then used to purchase housing, food, and clothing. However, there are certain tasks for which there is no payment, and these usually are the tasks considered to belong to women: cooking in the home, sewing in the home, cleaning the house, shopping, washing and ironing, looking after the children. In certain circumstances, such as when the family has enough money and/or the woman is "working" for a paycheck, some of these services may be purchased.

Looking back to the agricultural and preindustrial living and work situation, however, we find overall neither the male nor the female receiving a paycheck. The goods produced by both could be exchanged or sold for other goods. Similarly the farm family often does not run into the same difficulties in classifying "work" as does the family in which one or more adults must leave the home to "work" to collect a paycheck. On the farm each family member has a certain responsibility in producing the end product. The interdependencies are much more obvious to all involved. The woman working the farm is not perceived as isolated, protected, or set apart.

Another complication in the use of the word "work" is the selectivity imposed by some people in determining what is and what is not "work," even when a paycheck is involved. Is sitting at a desk "work"? Is thinking "work"? What about painting? playing music? praying? writing? preaching?

Identification of one's work often determines how one is treated. On the whole, women's work—does that phrase conjure up some specific images of what women do?—is considered to be that which is helpful to the man in performing his work. This connotation applies in both paid and unpaid work:

> The woman takes care of the home and the children so the man can go out to work.
>
> The woman is the nurse who makes possible the doctor's art of healing.
>
> The woman manages the office, answers the phone, handles correspondence and filing, so the man can conduct his decision-making tasks.
>
> The waitress serves the food necessary for the business luncheon or for the man to entertain a woman.

There are fallacies in these images, but the important thing is that the images do exist in our minds, and they affect our actions and our decisions. The biggest fallacy is the generalization that women are not normally miners, construction workers, or truck drivers, nor are they doctors or engineers, or business executives. Neither are men thought of as nurses or secretaries or teachers.

Statistically there are still few women in these positions and few men in the traditionally "female" jobs, except where the salaries have been considerably increased through collective bargaining, as in teaching. Until a few years ago men were all but a few of the college professors, but women made up most of the precollege teaching corps. In a restaurant that promotes itself as elegant one finds male waiters, not waitresses. And the idea of the ultimate chef is a male. But the cook is a female.

Civil rights legislation and affirmative action have broken some of the barriers to women entering the "male" world of work. One major step was the emphasis on schools accepting women into training programs: engineering, law, doctoral degree studies, medicine, dentistry. Although most schools now accept women as students, many still have few women faculty and few role models and support structures for the female student.

The trades are still relatively closed to women. The craft unions are traditionally male, and are comprised of family members. If you look at the membership lists in any given locale of a craft local, you will be amazed at the numbers of persons who have the same name. The crafts traditionally are passed from father to son, and so union membership follows this same pattern. The printers unions are one example of this; carpenters, electricians, plumbers, even drivers (Teamsters), follow similar habits.

On the whole, only when the courts have ordered changes in membership selection and apprenticeship selection do we find blacks and women as members of craft unions. To some extent the courts are also responsible for integration of the larger unions, such as the Auto Workers and Steelworkers and Mine Workers.

Women are members of all these unions now, and they have reached leadership positions in the United Auto Workers. Yet it was only in 1980 that the Executive

Council of the American Federation of Labor and Congress of Industrial Organizations selected a woman as a member for the first time. This woman is also president of the Coalition of Labor Union Women, an organization of union women subsidized by the AFL-CIO. There was much grumbling at the time of her selection that she is not a union president, and resistance to her being on the Executive Council.

The higher paid positions tend to be held by men, whether in the professions or in the trades. Even though women now hold close to 50 percent of all jobs, unions are slow to organize women, so ingrained are the biases and images that women's work really isn't work and that women are really not in the work force.

In a recent analysis of economic structures and directions in the United States, researchers found that in 1975—the last year for which industry-occupation breakdowns are available—women held 49 percent of the service jobs and 24 percent of the nonservice jobs. The occupational class of service worker includes cooks, housekeepers, cleaning workers, food service workers, and health service workers (not nurses). The number of service industry-occupational subgroups with higher than average female employment were all concentrated in earnings classes below $9,500: three in the $7,000–$9,499 class, fourteen in the $4,500–$6,999 class, and nine in the less than $4,500 class. Between 1970 and 1977, 31 percent of the job increases for women were in clerical positions; 28 percent in service positions; and 11 percent in crafts, sales, and laboring positions.

This research also notes that lower-income workers have minimal protections. They generally are not covered by collective bargaining agreements, grievance procedures, health and life insurance benefits, or affirmative action plans providing means for advancement. Nevertheless, educational requirements were found to be higher in the service positions than, for example, in manufacturing positions. Women workers have a high school diploma, and often some college, when earning an income comparable to that of a man with a grade school education.

Employment of women in the managerial category increased at a rate of 10 percent or more a year between 1970 and 1977. During this same period, nearly 20 percent of the increases in female jobs occurred in the occupational classifications, including professionals, technicians, and kindred workers. (Thomas M. Stanback, Jr., et al., *Services: The New Economy;* Allanheld, Osmun & Co., 1981.)

So, you may be thinking, women do now have the option of making their work in any field or any trade, if they are persistent and diligent, and willing to do whatever is necessary to succeed. While this is true, there are real difficulties facing women in the world of work outside the home. These should not be perceived as barriers, but they must be recognized and addressed, preferably with the support and help of the persons—both female and .nale—around the individual woman.

An integral part of working for a paycheck is money. Though this may not be the woman's only reason for working, the paycheck does measure her worth by the standards of the work world.

Many women are heads of households or live alone. They cannot survive without income from their work. Still they earn much less money than comparable males who are heads of households or who live alone. The majority of heads of households existing on incomes below the poverty level are women.

Money influences our decisions. It costs money to live. The Women's Bureau of the U.S. Department of Labor has documented over the years the low income of workingwomen, showing that money is a primary objective of most women who work outside the home. In 1978 they found the median wage or salary income of full-time workers to be:

minority women	$8,996	minority men	$12,885
white women	$9,578	white men	$16,194

Women with four years of college earned less on the average than men with an eighth-grade education. One in seven families was maintained by a woman in 1979, up from one in ten in 1969. Forty percent of black families were maintained by women. But three out of four *poor* black families were maintained by women. Of all poor families, half were maintained by women in 1979.

In 1979 about two thirds of the women in the labor force were single, widowed, divorced, or separated, or were married to men whose earnings were less than $10,000 in 1978. Fifty-five percent of the mothers with children under eighteen years of age were working in 1979; 45 percent of the mothers with preschool children were working. Sixty percent of all women aged eighteen to sixty-four were officially part of the work force in 1979.

MONEY AND POWER

Most women who work outside the home do need the money they earn to survive. Who are we to draw the line, for someone else, between needing money and wanting money? Nevertheless, some people in our society think women should not be working unless they need money, and they should not earn any more money than what they actually *need*. Somehow for men money can be, and is, a measure of status, so it is expected that they will want to make more and more money, whether or not they "need" it. The trade unions have negotiated higher and higher wages for workers, not based on workers' needs but on the value of the work within the context of the company and its profits. Managers are sometimes paid several hundred thousand dollars a year, not because they need the money. Few people question this income of managers. Many people are questioning union scale wages right now because of plant layoffs and closings and the high rate of unemployment. They also question women in the work force, taking up jobs "needed by men." There is inconsistency in the attitudes toward income, money, salaries and wages, and power when relating these to women and then to men.

A man is not asked why he is working. Probably no woman who works escapes the question why she is working. Some men and women are critical of women working instead of being at home looking after home and children; they are often just as critical of women or mothers on welfare who are at home taking care of their children.

We are conditioned to find these attitudes and inequities acceptable. We wonder inside whether we are not normal if we do not have a husband to support us. And we blame ourselves. This is a feeling that is difficult to overcome, for our reason tells us differently.

Status in our society is measured by money, but it is also measured by what we "do," which is usually defined as work. What power or influence do we have in our place of work? What is our sphere of control or responsibility? If it is the home or family, that is construed as woman's sphere of influence, and not on the hierarchy of power or status.

These perceptions and attitudes directly affect our mental and physical health. The source for our sense of self-worth, confidence, self-respect is all too often the reflection we get from those around us. If others don't take us seriously, or do not value our ideas, experience, and skills, we find it difficult to value them ourselves without becoming isolated from the world and people around us. When others do not value us, and we begin to lose our own sense of self, we become less and less able to function, even in the traditional world of women's work—homemaking, cooking, raising children.

What does all this mean to the Christian woman? And what does it mean to the Christian churches seeking to involve and serve women as an integral part of the church, the church family, and the church community?

The facts of the world of work have to be translated into terms that make it possible for a woman to integrate her daily life with her beliefs and the doctrines of the Christian church, i.e., to be a whole person. The word "work" needs to be broadened to cover all that one does in and with one's life. What one does with one's life truly must reflect one's understanding of God's will and a responsiveness to God's love and calling. It is this direction which makes it possible for us to work, wherever that work may be, and to grow and survive as a person. The Twenty-third Psalm, known so well to us all, conveys this message:

> The LORD is my shepherd, I shall not want;
>   he makes me lie down in green pastures.
> He leads me beside still waters;
>   he restores my soul.
> He leads me in paths of righteousness
>   for his name's sake.
>
> (Ps. 23:1–3)

Each of us has the gift of being. We also have the freedom to choose what to do with that being, that life. Should we not use that gift to multiply the gifts which God has given to us? And what does that mean in our daily life? How shall we live? Where shall we live? With whom shall we live? What shall we do? How shall we spend our time?

The horizons of possibilities are far beyond our human sight. For each of us the response and the decision must be different, and perhaps different from day to day and year to year. Still it is to God that we can and must respond. That is the inner direction of our souls, vital to wholeness, peace, and happiness.

Most people probably do not consider work decisions in the light of a Christian vocation, except when the decisions relate to religious professions or jobs. But work decisions reflect values, priorities, material wants, time commitments, status in relationships with other people, personal fulfillment and satisfaction, family commitments, and power needs. At times we don't have a wide range of choice in making work decisions, but overall we do have a say in how much and what education we obtain, the type of work we seek, how we function in the work situation, how we spend our nonwork hours, how many hours we work, our community involvement, where we live, and our financial and family commitments.

God has given us freedom and responsibility. Most of us can do better in exercising our freedom in a thoughtful, responsive, caring, loving way. As we move through the chapters of this book, work should take on a renewed meaning and the idea of committing our life to God should take on the challenge and depth of his promise to us:

> Blessed be the name of God for ever and ever,
> to whom belong wisdom and might.
> He changes times and seasons;
> he removes kings and sets up kings;

he gives wisdom to the wise
and knowledge to those who have
understanding;
he reveals deep and mysterious things;
he knows what is in the darkness,
and the light dwells with him.

(Dan. 2:20–22)

CHAPTER 2

Work as a Life Goal

VOCATION

Throughout the centuries religious persons have written about dedication of one's life to God. A continuing thesis in Christian reform movements has been responsiveness to and reflection on God's will and word. The evangelical movements removed the priest as intermediary, so to allow direct communication between the individual person and God, hence individual interpretations and expression. Vatican II probably had its greatest impact in turning the Mass into a celebration to be shared almost totally by the congregation. The Mass was translated into "native" languages so everyone could understand the words being spoken; laypersons were authorized to read the Lesson. The "mysteries" became more those of the Spirit, and less the terrain of the priesthood. Today several Catholic theologians encourage individual prayer, meditation, reception of the Holy Spirit, without the intermediaries of the past.

If one is to view life as a gift of God, and then to dedicate that life to God and God's service, one must have some means of "hearing," of communication, and of responding. That means of communicating will differ according to the individual's religious faith, but the given remains—that the individual person has the ability to believe, and the freedom to choose. With that freedom comes the responsibility to choose what is right. And in the Christian view, what is right is what is God's way, God's will.

This choice can be in any sphere. We tend to think of work as something nonreligious. Yet work is what we do with our time, even when we "play." Why should this fall into the religious arena? you ask. Think about it: work—whatever we do with the bulk of our time—consumes more hours and energy than any other single thing in our lives. Therefore, if we intend to dedicate our lives to God, we need to be able to dedicate our work to God. If we cannot, we will not be at peace with ourselves, with our family, with our neighbors, with our God.

How many people do you know who dislike their jobs; have difficulty getting up in the morning because they have to go to work; watch the clock all day and wish the days away; are grumpy in the morning and withdrawn by the time they come home at night? Can they be experiencing, and sharing, the love of God? Are these not the same people who often question people who do not "work"—people on welfare, artists, academics, theologians, persons who give their lives to prayer? It is almost as though for some people the definition of work is suffering; that if one obtains satisfaction, even joy, from work, and one involves one's being in work, then it no longer qualifies as "work."

Do you wonder why people—men and women—stay in work situations when they seem to be so unhappy? Are you such a person? Oftentimes people who are really discouraged do not have the strength to change their situation, or even to think through what is wrong and try to correct it. Change can be extremely difficult. This applies even to the mother coping with the departure of grown children and the empty house.

Yet we can always change in many ways. No matter what our situation or long-term commitments and responsibilities, we can change, we have choices to make. These can be the most creative moments in our lives, but only if we decide to consider the options. We must let our imaginations and dreams run free. We must be still and listen, be open, be ready to respond to any opportunity or challenge, no matter how difficult or overwhelming it may seem. This is the "leap of faith," beyond what reason may tell us.

Let us look at ourselves for a moment. When do we get discouraged? Never when we feel we are giving of ourselves and sharing love. Discouragement is emptiness, isolation, coldness. We experience discouragement when we cut ourselves off from God's love, when we are hurt by a loved one, when we begin to do our work without involving ourselves, when we feel shunned by those to whom we are trying to give.

Do your children care whether or not you prepare their dinner? Does your supervisor care whether or not you do your work accurately and thoroughly? Does it matter whether or not you volunteer your time and skills to your church? And so on.

The key is, how do you feel about it? Do *you* care? Does it matter to *you*? If not, then you need to examine carefully what you are doing, how, and why. Do you believe in what you are doing? Is it "right" for you, for your life, for your vocation? If not, don't you owe it to yourself, and to those around you and to God, to change? to seek out what *is* right?

No matter how we may try otherwise, work *is* integral to our lives. And so it must be integral to our faith. This includes being a volunteer in whatever capacity, maintaining a home and family, performing tasks for an employer for pay. Since faith must live, so must our work be alive to us. And to be alive is to change. With change come stress, anxiety, fear, but also the potential for greater happiness, joy, fulfillment.

To have a vocation is to have a calling. Most of us have heard of men, and sometimes women, having a calling to the ministry or to missionary work. The word "vocation," though, is now usually used to refer to trades, as in "vocational education" and "vocational schools." But for us vocation will have the more literal meaning of a *calling*. This vocation is our lifework. Our vocation, therefore, is a reflection of our faith, of our following God's will.

Remember for a moment those who question people who do not work, taking the narrow view of work. Then think for a moment about Jesus' life. Did he ever "work"? It seems all he did was go out and talk with people, heal people, and travel around a lot. And to top this, he told people to give up their possessions and follow him around. How did they previously get their worldly possessions except mainly by work and sale of products? Jesus told them to give up their present work and way of life and to believe in him, to follow him, wherever that might be. He didn't tell them much about where they would be going, or what they would be doing.

Most of us would not want to act on such vagueness, but that is the level of faith Jesus asks of us. We must at least try to follow. To begin that process, then, let us take on the use of this word "vocation" as our life goal, our lifework.

Our vocation can be anything, or any mix of things. We know that every society needs artists and musicians and writers, government leaders, tradespeople to make and to fix things, people to raise and educate children, people to grow and distribute food, people to build and sell homes, people to handle the exchange of money or goods, and so on. Who performs these tasks, and under what circumstances and for what benefits, is what varies, as does the value placed on each of these tasks. Herein lies the freedom of choice, individual fulfillment, individual responsibility. Yet whatever one does must be that person's vocation.

In a rather interesting perversion of these interrelationships and tasks women have come to carry the responsibility for performing certain tasks, and men others, with men usually receiving greater worldly remuneration. Yet both women and men require housing, food, and clothing. Why should women regularly be paid much less than men? There is no reason for this unfairness.

Yet many of us women have accepted injustice, ending up with a low expectation of ourselves, assuming we could do little with our lives. Strange how what could be a positive value of dedication and commitment could end up within a social/economic structure to be harmful to the potential, even the personhood, of women. This perhaps more than anything is the conflict we as women need to address. We need to make our vocational decisions free from the biases and expectations of the people and the world around us while at the same time living and functioning in that world. We can dedicate ourselves and have vocations in ways very different from the roles of wife, mother, nurse, teacher, helper. First we have to believe in our own potential, and then we can begin to teach those around us. On a parallel we also have to encourage men to consider a variety of roles, including being a full-time husband and father.

The women's movement has helped us to see the options, widened our horizons. It has helped open doors to let us enter. One crucial question we as women now seem to face is whether we must give up the qualities and satisfactions of our traditional roles to succeed in what is generally known as the work world. Or, can we bring to the world of work a caring and loving that would make our work truly our vocation? Can we help temper the aggressiveness expected of the business person with the qualities of a loving mother? Is it not possible to be a whole, caring person no matter what one's work? I believe that it is. It is the dimension that Christian women can add to the world of work.

Rather than becoming hard and tough we must hold our own for being whole persons, and treating customers and other workers as whole persons, caring about them and being fair, honest, and helpful. Sometimes I wonder if we should not back up and ask why we have government and why we have business and why we have money and an economy. Is it not so that people can live, and that to the fullest of their potential? If this were our goal, I think women would manage better throughout the world of work.

Too often, however, there is a good deal of pressure on all employees to conform, to be "loyal," to compete where competition is fostered, to get into the power games. When a woman does not fit into these, whether by choice or by her nature, she becomes suspect and is sidelined.

The wholeness of a human being is fragile, and so easily cracked and broken. Our vocation is what makes us whole, and keeps us whole. Yet the realities of daily living and working have many effects on our attaining our goals. Exercising freedom, especially within the framework of vocation and faith, is hard work. One must constantly question, and spend time thinking, reading, meditating, and praying in an effort to be clear of the details and stress of the immediate world around. But the reward is the most wonderful gift ever.

WOMEN AND THE IDEA OF VOCATION

The critical first step for the young woman seeking her vocation is to believe, to have faith, to know that she has the freedom of choice. If she believes this and can go ahead and collect information on alternatives and examine it, she is creating for herself the real possibility of choice. How she chooses will in large part be affected by:

What she thinks of herself. Does she believe she is able to learn new skills, to take on challenges that she hasn't tried, to move into unfamiliar places and experiences? Does she see herself as being an entity, or does she feel that she needs to be attached to, an extension of, another person? Does she feel able to be herself, or does she need to reflect others, and others' opinions?

What she thinks she is capable of. Does she look objectively at her aptitudes and skills and abilities? Has she even tried enough different things to have a reasonable grasp of what she is capable of? Can she reach outside and beyond herself to see and do different, new things, learn new skills?

What others think she is capable of. Does she sense from those around her that there are specific roles for her and she cannot, should not, move beyond these? Is she told by parents, teachers, friends that she does not have the ability to become a member of a trade or a profession? Are her dreams denied by those around her, and does this cause her to lose faith?

What her family expects of her. What has her family communicated to her as her goal in life? How do they expect her to pursue this? Is there pressure on her to marry and have children? Does her mother need grandchildren to look after to help her feel needed and wanted?

Money. What is her means of support? Will her family send her to school? Can she live at home? Does she need money to pay all, or part, of her living expenses? Does she have the time to be able to learn a trade or a profession and still have the money to survive?

Living status and needs. What are her actual survival needs? What living options does she have, and therefore what cost options? Can she live simply and inexpensively, or does she think she needs to maintain a "higher" standard of living? Does she dress simply and inexpensively? Does she eat nourishing, but not expensive, foods? Does she take advantage of free leisure activities?

Availability of schools and training programs. What is available that is nearby, or in a place where she can live inexpensively (unless her parents can pay her living expenses while she is in training or school)? Does she have the credentials to be accepted into schools or programs she wants to attend? Is she familiar with schools or programs that offer a variety of training and educational skills? Do her interests and aptitudes fit what she knows is available, or can she search out what she needs to move toward a specialty or career?

Availability of jobs. What is the job market? Will there be jobs at the end of the training or education? Are there jobs that she can hold while becoming trained? Can she make enough money to live and still go to school?

Involvement in a church and the attitudes within that church toward women. Does her church support her in her dreams, her plans to follow a vocation? Or does the church communicate to her a more narrow direction for her role in life? What expectations do the members of the parish have for her? What support do they give her? What barriers do they create?

Availability of support and acceptance from others. Are there people in her life who encourage her to follow her vocation? to move into areas that interest her? to try to find ways to make her dreams come true? When she hits a roadblock, do they help her to work it through and to keep on going?

Personal health. Does she have any limitations caused by personal health that must be considered, i.e., climate, mobility, stress, endurance?

Health of close family and friends. Does she have time commitments to caring for persons close to her that must be taken into account in planning training, education, career, or job?

Emotional needs. What type of situation does she need to be productive and effective? Does she need to be allowed to work on her own, to be creative, to be close to fellow workers, to see an end product, to make others feel better?

Values. What does she need to accomplish to feel good about herself and what she is doing? What experiences reinforce her and give her the energy to move on? What rewards does she need to be motivated to carry on, and to continue to pursue her vocation? What results does she need to see?

Given the above factors and their influence on decision-making, we may logically conclude that any decision-making about a job, or about education and training, needs to include review of the following questions:

What are my financial needs—for housing, food, clothing, transportation? Which are needs, which

are wants, and why? What are my psychological
and emotional needs for acceptance and status?

What are my needs for power, over people, and over
things?

What are my needs for personal satisfaction and
fulfillment?

What situations make me uncomfortable?

What are my time priorities?

What are my commitments to people—family, community, friends?

How consuming do I want or need my job to be in
terms of my total life?

What values do I need to have reflected in my work
or my work situation?

What are my life goals and how can my work help me
to achieve them?

Most of us cannot answer all these questions with any
thoroughness. Many of the answers are the things we
learn about ourselves over a lifetime. And they change as
we change, and grow. Still the questions must be asked
to spur on our thinking and our analysis, to help us to
make decisions that reflect who we are and where we are
trying to go. The difficult part is keeping our minds open
to change, to opportunities, and to challenge.

Upon completing high school most young women
consider either just getting a job or going on to school. A
few get married. A couple of decades ago marriage was
the first step. At that time few trades or professional
schools would even consider women applicants.

Choosing a career or postsecondary education or training at age sixteen or seventeen can be little more than
guesswork. Choice of a college is likely to be determined
by geographical location and distance, cost, size, and
some general curriculum offerings. Once in a school an
individual can broaden her horizons in discovering the

possible, and then can move somewhat freely among majors.

How free we are to move has a lot to do with the level of our self-confidence. In our late teens, and later, most of us are not at all sure who we are, and so we tend to take upon ourselves the definitions, attitudes, expectations of those around us. If a school does not encourage women students to take mathematics or engineering or physics, then we either agree to not taking these courses or decide to prove we can do it. If your faith, your conviction, your confidence is strong, you will go ahead and do what seems right, and you will have a good chance of success. It is when we do not believe in ourselves, and our abilities, that we tend to set ourselves up for failure.

At the same time that she is working through her training, career, or job direction, a young woman is faced with vocational decisions about having a family. As she matures sexually, she must consciously make some long-range decisions about her relationships with men, her sexual behavior, and her desire to have, or not to have, children. Integral to these decisions is the decision to, or not to, marry, and the circumstances or conditions under which she does marry. There is little encouragement in our society to consider these issues and questions in an informed and rational manner. These are matters of the heart.

But as we all learn eventually, much more than emotions is involved in marriage and in having and raising children. And we find how volatile are our emotions. Marriage and lifetime commitments involve so much more than the love we think we have for a person at age nineteen or twenty.

The lack of information in the home, in schools, and in churches about sex, marriage, and child-rearing limits the availability of information to young women and to young men. Once a young woman becomes pregnant, and/or marries, she has already made a lifetime decision and is faced with a whole different set of responsibilities and choices from those she faced before marriage and/or pregnancy.

Most churches, and society generally, place the primary value for the woman on marriage and motherhood. They also tend to place the responsibility for the home and family on the woman. The image of Mary as mother is still influential throughout the Christian churches. Joseph, as father, has a minimal role, especially since promulgation by the Roman Catholic Church of the doctrine of the virgin birth.

The young woman active in a parish is likely automatically to assume marriage and children are her real goal in life, her vocation. She may well never consider these as one part of her lifework, or as one of several alternatives. If she is then, or later, unhappy or unfulfilled, she is likely to blame herself. This guilt in turn only increases her unhappiness and inability to be open and responsive to those around her, and to God.

I remember vividly how I felt as a teenager completing high school and then starting college. I thought I should be getting married, or at least be going steady with the person I would marry. I felt like such an outsider, such a failure. What was the matter with me?

I had no idea whatsoever of what was involved in marriage or in raising children. Meanwhile, I tried to go about my studies, without any sense of confidence or direction, since I had failed in what was most important. I in no way saw myself as a whole person. How could I be whole outside of marriage, or at least without a steady male partner?

I needed a vocation, but I was floundering and found nowhere to turn. The women's movement helped me begin to sort out what was real and what were pressures imposed from outside, but the dimension of faith was missing.

The churches can offer so much to women in helping them to sort out who they are, their vocation, their options, and the barriers they encounter.

The narrow view of women reflected traditionally in the Christian churches is carried over to the employer. Up until 1970 it was not uncommon to hear employers express concern about hiring a young woman because she would just get married and leave. Or the reason given for not hiring a woman in a professional position or in a job with a progression for advancement would be that the employer would be giving the woman all the training, would become dependent on her, and then she would get pregnant or her husband would be transferred. Employers were not entirely inaccurate in this perception. Our own attitudes toward ourselves, ignoring our own economic needs and actual work behavior, reflected this same perception of women workers.

We find it difficult to develop a sense of self, and, with that, self-confidence and a sense of self-worth. Yet, taken rationally, how can we enter into a marriage partnership, or even know ourselves in some relationship to God, when we cannot believe in the existence of our own self? We cannot make choices if we are not in some degree whole. We cannot grow if there is not a seed to sprout and be nourished, which dependent though it is on its environment, still exists as an independent seed.

If we constantly put ourselves down and box ourselves in, we severely stunt our potential. The self must have sunshine, fertile soil, and loving care, but not just from the outside. This development and nurturing of the self as integral to vocation is not a selfishness, so abominable to most women, or selflessness. Both words seem without meaning in this context. The self is a reflection of God's love.

THE SELF

Who am I? That age-old question is responsible for much deep pondering. But this question has also led individuals to a belief in God and in a spiritual unity of individual persons. It is a question of chaos and at the same time a question of faith. It can also be a question of knowing oneself. Who am I? What can I do? What do I want to do? What do I have to offer? to whom? What is my potential? What physical, psychological, and emotional needs do I have? What situations am I comfortable in? When and where do I feel estranged? Who are the people closest to me? Why?

Sometimes knowing ourselves seems an impossibility. Too often it seems we can recognize ourselves more easily in hindsight than in a present situation. This makes decision-making rather difficult. Knowing what is essential to one's well-being comes slowly. What we think we need, and what we really need, may be two different things. Or, what we think is most important to us may end up not being important at all.

This learning to know oneself comes the same way as any other learning: watching and studying ourselves. It may be the most important studying we ever do, for it can determine our ability to make decisions which are right for us.

To complicate things even further, we are not static. We are alive, growing, changing, developing, responding to people and to situations and to the world around us. What hurts one day may cause happiness later. What seems marvelous at the time may have unforeseen bad effects.

The human being is a complex subject, and bears sensitive and compassionate attention to detail. Knowledge comes only with such a careful approach. Too often we do not study ourselves enough, a subject that ought to equal any other in importance.

We do not exist alone, so who we are to some extent involves also whom we associate with, whom we identify as role models, whom we seek out as friends. The people around us and the situations and surroundings we are in have much to do with molding us as persons. Philosophers, psychologists, sociologists, theologians have discussed for centuries the various factors that build the self, and ways to define the self. This discussion should never end.

The most important others in our lives are usually the adults who raise us. We may accept, reject, modify the behavior and the values we take on from these adults, but we do, nevertheless, react in some way to goals and models presented to us. We need to identify consciously these goals which have been internalized, for this will help us better understand our own actions and reactions.

In working out what is most important to us as persons, we need to determine what is most important to those around us, partly just so we understand their reactions to us and our own values.

A recent poll of two thousand children, male and female, found their top thirty heroes to all be entertainers or sports figures, only five of whom were women. Girls apparently still do not have female role models or heroes or heroines after whom to model themselves or to form their dreams. The imagination of the child needs some content with which to create realistic ideas of self.

Within the Christian framework the self is defined generally as that which God has created. A oneness, yet part of a whole, through God. Separate, distinct, yet part of the One who is all Creation. The self includes all that is the individual person from the physical body to the mind, feelings, emotions, thoughts. For the individual self to thrive, it must be in tune with the Whole, and likewise all the parts of the self must be in tune with each other. When the self is out of tune, then it ceases to grow, and be healthy, and discouragement, unhappiness, anger, and frustration may set in.

The self is fragile. It is buffeted by the world around, and by all the exchanges with other people and involvement in various situations. But the strength of the self comes with knowledge of that self, and with the ability to be, to be at one with oneself and with one's God.

The search for one's self is treacherous; it is also inspiring. Perhaps to find one's self is to find God. Some theologians and philosophers have suggested such an inward route. One must pray and meditate as well as study. The saints more than any other persons have found peace, direction, knowledge. Some became actively involved in the world with a clear purpose; others wrote or shared their direction with other persons. Still they seem to have found their goals and a way to work toward them that made it possible for them to function in the world yet have contact with themselves, and with God.

Jesus' second commandment directs us to love our neighbor as ourselves. If we don't love ourselves, can we then love our neighbor? or God? If I do not love myself, can I receive God's love?

Knowledge and love of oneself would appear to be essential to love, to life itself, as one intends to live by God's will. Yet we do little to help and nurture that self, or the self in others. We need the support of our churches in pursuing this goal. And we need to support each other. Women's groups have tried to provide the help required, but we still need to find the nurturing love in our church family.

Finding one's vocation or life goal is a lifelong search. We need structures within our churches to help us along the way, even though the decisions must be very personal and individual.

Following are some questions to help you take the first steps in preparing your life plan, which itself must be constantly changing to reflect your growth. In later chapters we shall consider more specifically the narrower decision-making relating to job, volunteering, marriage and family, and values.

> What is important to me?
> What is essential to my being happy?
> What is essential to my survival and growth as a person?
> Where or in what do I find fulfillment?
> What do I need to ensure I have time to do?
> What options do I want and need to consider in developing my life plan?
>> with people
>> with job
>> with community
>> with church

CHAPTER 3

Woman in the Workplace— Part I

The choice is yours. But is it? Can you, a woman, choose what career you want to seek? Can you be accepted as a trade apprentice, as a medical student, as a musician or a theologian? Can you choose both family and career? Can you, should you, find your work, and your fulfillment, as wife-mother-and-volunteer?

What are your values and your life goals? Who and what do you want to be? Can you really try to achieve these goals? Will your family and friends understand and love you if you pursue your life goals? Will you be alone? Will you be a failure if you do not marry; or if you do marry and do not have children?

What does your church say to you? What options do you have as a woman? Within your personal religious framework, what do you think of yourself as a woman? Who are you?

Most of the hierarchies in the world we live in are male. Every major corporation president, and most, if not all, of the board members, are men. Most government officials are men. Nearly all ministers, and all priests, are men. Store managers and restaurant managers are still mainly men. Hospital board members and doctors and dentists and pharmacists and lawyers are predominantly men. Tradespeople and repair personnel are nearly all men. But we know that women make up nearly 50 percent of the official work force. In this chapter we shall be looking at women in the workplace itself and the roles women play in the more narrowly focused world of employment for pay.

THE LAW

We women are still in a way second-class citizens. We were given the vote only in this century. Although in the past decade the federal courts have interpreted the Constitution to say women are equal to men, particularly in the employment arena, the fight for the Equal Rights Amendment is lost for the present. One must ask why. What is the controversy? Why is it so important to so many people to spend so much money to oppose the ERA? If all the proposed amendment does is state that under the Constitution of the United States, women are equal to men (and we believe that each of us is a child of God equal to all other children of God), then what is to be so feared by passage of the ERA? The only conclusion that occurs to me is that women are still in fact not to be allowed to be equal. And certainly some churches do teach the inequality of women. Various theological positions are presented for this view.

Despite the failure of passage of the Equal Rights Amendment many legal steps have been taken in the past few years to establish the equality of the female worker to the male worker.

The most momentous of these is the 1964 Civil Rights Act as amended in 1974 to include prohibition of sex discrimination. The 1967 Equal Pay Act has been used extensively to implement the principle of equal pay for equal work. Several states and units of local government have adopted a variety of legislation prohibiting sex discrimination in employment, training, education, and housing. More recently the Congress adopted the Education Equity Act and the Equality in Credit Act. Some of the most important precedent-setting actions by government, however, have been taken under state and federal administrative executive orders that provide for a network of affirmative action and "contract compliance."

The administrative structures that resulted from the legislation and the executive orders that penetrate the entire economic structure of the country are the U.S. Equal Employment Opportunity Commission (EEOC), the U.S. Office of Federal Contract Compliance (OFCC), and local human relations commissions.

The EEOC has the authority and responsibility to take complaints of discrimination, investigate the facts, propose solutions, and, if not satisfied by the response of the employer, take legal action. In the late 1960s the EEOC began initiating class-action suits against major employers who perpetrated systemic discrimination, usually on the basis of both race and sex. The grounds for these class-action suits were the numbers: numbers of people in each job class by race and sex, salary or wage level by race and sex and job class, hiring practices, use of employment tests that had unequal effects by race and sex and were not valid, childbirth leave practices, and so on. The EEOC presented numbers showing patterns and practices of discrimination that were upheld in the federal courts, with the courts deciding *not* to consider whether or not there was *intent* to discriminate.

The court cases had a far-ranging impact in changing the world of work for women. The investigative process for individual complaints had proved to be detrimental to the complainant by placing the burden of proof of discrimination on the victim, the complainant. In the final agreements or court orders resulting from the class-action suits claiming system discrimination, employers such as Bell Telephone were required to develop and to implement affirmative action plans with specific hiring and promotion goals and objectives. The intent of this affirmative action approach was to redress past wrongs, to make the extra effort to ensure equal opportunity, and to examine all personnel practices to eliminate any that had a discriminatory effect.

Some of the discriminatory practices identified and documented by the EEOC in these cases are:

No advertisement of vacant positions in general circulation publications, or in publications targeted to women or minority groups

Requirements for applicants that were not relevant to job performance (i.e., height requirements for a police officer; college degree)

Unequal application of eligibility requirements, such as not counting a woman's education or experience as equal to those of a man, and often requiring higher levels of education from a female applicant

Use of all-white male trade unions for hiring referrals

Forced resignation because of pregnancy

Forced resignation of the female employee if a relationship developed between male and female employee that violated company policy

Refusal to hire a woman if traveling were involved

Refusal to hire a woman if the position required communicating directly with managerial or executive type people who were all men

Directing interview questions to the woman's sex life, family plans, child responsibilities

Channeling women into certain positions and men into others, thus creating a sex-segregated work force and job classes, with the female positions usually involving much lower pay and fewer benefits and opportunities for advancement

The settlements to these class-action suits contained several common elements, which today are generally considered essential to good personnel practices:

Validation of all selection criteria and procedures to ensure that more female and minority applicants are not being excluded than are white male applicants. This can be accomplished through statistical analyses, or more simply by monitoring selection results.

Aggressive recruitment of qualified minority and female applicants. In some cases this simply meant allowing women and minority candidates to submit an application for a position heretofore held only by white males.

Career ladders as an integral part of the overall personnel system, including provision of relevant training and experience.

Increased employer training, with less dependence on general degrees, licenses, or apprenticeships, which historically have excluded women and minority persons from their programs.

Hiring and promotion goals and timetables (the most controversial part of affirmative action). The purpose is to make the employer set a goal that must be met, no matter what it takes. This practice eliminates efforts to hide behind the excuse that there are no qualified women, and it heightens the importance of effective recruiting, of valid selection criteria, of establishing career ladders.

Childbirth, not pregnancy, leave, which does not penalize a woman for bearing and rearing children. (The concept of leave for the father, and

flexibility for parents to care for their children, is
coming much more slowly.)

Flextime, part time, working at home, on-site child
care are beginning to be used by a few employers
for all workers, but much of the discussion around
these supports and flexibility resulted from efforts
to equalize opportunities, given the societal re-
quirement that women raise the children.

Just because these are considered good personnel
practices does not mean that they are followed by every
employer. Those most likely to comply are the larger
employers who also have government contracts. It was
the Office of Federal Contract Compliance which put the
teeth into affirmative action, often in response to wom-
en's rights and civil rights organizations and threatened
legal action. Some industries actually lost government
contracts, and many others changed some of their practices as the result of on-site investigations. Recently,
however, this thrust has been curtailed as part of the
program to "get government off our backs." Still many
employers have seen the benefits in more equal employment practices through improved morale and productivity, and several are still under court order.

The present legal battle lines were drawn by the
EEOC under Eleanor Holmes Norton with the issue of
equivalent work for comparable or equivalent pay. Under the Equal Pay Act the complainant has to show *equal*
work for unequal pay. The argument now being raised is
whether women in one position doing work *equivalent*
to men in another position should receive the same pay.
This issue is the result of employers tending to classify
positions differently for women and men though the job
content may be basically the same.

For example, a major urban newspaper found itself
facing the following questions of equivalent pay:

Is a woman telephone advertising salesperson in any
way equal to the male outside salesperson, classi-
fied or display?

Is a female clerk handling payroll equal to a male
clerk handling the dispatch (not supervision) of
messengers?

Is the secretary to the president equal to a truck
driver?

Is the female accountant equal to a truck driver?

Then there arose the questions of what positions a
woman could handle if given the opportunity:

Can a woman do advertising artwork?

Can a woman handle computer terminals for setting
type?

Can a woman do heavy cleaning?

Can a woman be a printer?

Can a woman be a truck driver?

Can a woman recruit and manage news delivery
boys and girls?

Can a woman be a fore*man*?

The pattern of sex-segregated job classes was encouraged by the trade unions as they organized the men in
the workplace and negotiated higher pay scales for these
men and these job classes. Several trade unions refused
to allow women or minority persons as members until
well into the '60s. The result was that the employer tried
to retain control over the female job classes and to keep
the pay low. The lines between job classes became rigid,
with the unions controlling all referrals for jobs in some
positions covered by collective bargaining.

OUR OWN EXPECTATIONS

Though discrimination on the basis of sex is illegal in the workplace, we all know it exists. No one of us is unaffected by the world around us. When that world in various ways tells us that there are certain roles and behaviors expected, and others not allowed, to disobey these strictures is both difficult and emotionally draining.

Until about a decade ago women were often portrayed in history books, in reading books in school, and in the media as weak, as second to men, as homemakers, mothers, and wives, as romantic, as helpers—not as leaders or doers. With the development of the women's movement this portrayal of women is changing, though slowly.

When we look around us, we see women as:

> the secretary to the male executive (though we can now find the female executive and the male secretary)
>
> the nurse assisting the male doctor (though, again, we can now find the female doctor and the male nurse)
>
> the teacher of children (For a long time women taught the lower grades, with men being found in high schools and colleges; with representation of teachers by collective bargaining and the resultant higher pay scales many more men are found throughout the teaching profession.)
>
> nurse's aides
> receptionists and other clerical workers
> food service workers
> store clerks

maids in hotels
waitresses
human service workers (though in the professional
categories there are now probably nearly as many
men as women)
volunteers, mothers, housekeepers

We are beginning to see more women as:

bus drivers and taxicab drivers
workers on road construction crews, though mainly
as flag "men"
police officers, beat and desk
prison guards
truck drivers
machine operators, plumbers, electricians, carpenters
doctors, lawyers, dentists, pharmacists, engineers
elected officials

Although women are beginning to assume roles in a broader segment of the economy than in years past, moving into a nontraditional position is not easy. The assumptions made by colleagues, friends, and probably yourself are that you are not normal, that you are trying to "rise above your place in life." This puts you under extreme psychological pressure to succeed, and in some way to prove yourself.

This is probably the most difficult part of accepting the freedom of choice, the freedom to fulfill oneself and one's goals. The battle is fought within oneself as much as without. And that battle is to know oneself, to keep in tune with oneself, to avoid reflecting the characteristics imposed from the outside. This strength can come from nowhere else but through an inner peace, which in our Christian context can be attained only through prayer or meditation, oneness with the Spirit of God.

Loneliness and aloneness are two different things. Aloneness is something that we must know if we are to be able to live as a full person. It is difficult to imagine a person more alone than Jesus. Yet it is equally difficult to imagine him being lonely, so long as he was one with God the Father. Jesus tells us frequently, as do the prophets in the Old Testament, to stand alone. Don't go with the crowd. Don't follow the statutes that violate the laws of God. Don't do something, or try to be something, just because someone else is, or someone tells you to.

We all learn that when we try to be other than ourselves, it doesn't work for long. We become depressed, unhappy, unloving, separated from those about whom we do care.

During my work life I have found myself a number of times in positions where I was not expected to be effective. I have never quite been able to figure out why I was hired in the first place, unless it was that I appeared to be safe and would help the employer meet affirmative action goals. I am very serious about my work, whatever it may be, and have that female trait of having to do a superb job, no matter the cost to me.

The result was that I would throw my energies and skills and imagination into the situation and produce the results my employers said they wanted, only to be greeted with some applause, a good deal of hostility, jealousy from colleagues, and an increased work load. I felt good about what I accomplished, especially when I could see the impact on the lives of people I was trying to reach.

My undoing was the final realization that any change I managed to bring about would be temporary, lasting only so long as those committed to serving people remained in positions of control. I found I did not have the strength or the energy to maintain the changes against the forces of opposition and for the status quo. And I did not have the patience, nor again the energy, to chip away, taking a tiny step at a time.

The good part is that I can still see some positive results from every job, every project, on which I worked, from eliminating sexism in the schools to providing equal employment opportunity for women to setting up community centers for older people to developing alternatives to institutions for persons of all ages and conditions. I could not withstand the forces in the work world, but others came along who could take parts of what was prepared and carry it through. And the other side of all this is that it is important that any programs or service be owned by those who are to benefit, and only when the control is totally decentralized in terms of daily functions can this happen.

But we need more middle ground. We as women need ways to be renewed, to find sustenance, and to be sustenance to each other. We are alone in the work world, no matter what role we play. Just as the church has helped women isolated at home to be supportive of each other and to have time together, the church can help women in the work world to cope, to survive as persons, and to grow. I don't think it is possible to do it alone.

In all our approaches to the world of work we are confronted with the internal question, What is a woman? Am I to be mother first, or wife first, or employee first? But then we have to ask, Why do we even ask those questions? We do carry guilt about our inner perceptions of what our role in life is. Many of us over*do* both at home and in the work world. We think we have to do everything at home to make up for going out and working, even though we have to work for money. And we think we have to succeed in everything we do at work, to justify our being hired in the first place. This guilt must be recognized and addressed. Again the church could be so helpful in bringing women together to work through this guilt and our reactions to it. Our families would probably be much healthier if we could get past this guilt.

How many of us find it easier to go ahead and do all the dishes, and the laundry, and the cleaning, and the gardening, and take out the rubbish, and do the shopping, rather than to hassle (from our view) with our husband or child to take on a fair share? We say to ourselves, my husband has his work. What we have to internalize is that we have our work, too, and it is important, just as is the man's, and the child's. We shall look at this more fully later on, but in viewing our expectations of ourselves we have to remember the impact of our own guilt feelings.

The guilt in the workplace is emphasized by the present high rate of unemployment, plant shutdowns, and cuts in government spending in the community. How many times do you hear that women, and older people too, should give up their jobs so that no men would be unemployed? This ignores the statistics on women workers, but it has a real psychological effect on the woman worker.

As women we have to come to expect to be treated as equals, and to be respected. A few years ago this expectation was thought to be "uppity." Now it is essential for the woman worker to be able to function in the workplace. When she lets go of her own expectation for equality and respect, she will be beaten down. After all, if we don't value ourselves and our skills and abilities, how can we expect our co-workers or our employer to? We have to learn to behave as though we believe in ourselves and we expect equal opportunity and equal treatment, and we have earned respect.

Taking a look at almost any workplace, we can find situations in which women have not been able to convey an expectation of equality:

The men have their regular business lunches; the
women in the same position are not included, and
they do not build an equivalent structure (usually
they are too few, or only one).

The men have a company car, not the women.

The men have credit cards for entertaining, not the
women.

The men can take extended lunch hours without
anything being said, not the women.

The men can dress as they wish, not the women.

The situations vary, of course, from place to place, and
there are times when it appears the women get extra
privileges.

We accept all kinds of inequities, from not receiving
equal pay (we half believe we shouldn't) to not having an
opportunity for advancement to not having a chance to do
the more interesting work. We make all kinds of excuses
to ourselves as to why the men should have the better
chances and benefits, for we do not believe in ourselves.
And we have different expectations of women supervisors than of male supervisors. We let men get away with
almost anything.

Overall, we expect much more of ourselves—of wom-
en—than we do of men, and in a way we teach men to
have that same "over" expectation. There is a tendency
for the women in the nontraditional position to oversuc-
ceed and overproduce. And the male boss seems all too
willing to keep piling on the work and the expectations.
This results in failure on two fronts for the individual
woman: she becomes so overworked that she does not
function well and cannot take on any more; and, her co-
workers resent her working so hard and perhaps doing a
better job than they. Usually in such a situation neither
the woman nor the employer is consciously aware of
what is happening.

In some ways a woman must prove herself no matter what the nontraditional position she enters, but she must do this in a manner acceptable to herself, and to the men around her, without destroying herself. The woman in the construction gang faces the same pressures as the woman executive, and probably more aggressively and more openly. She does not go through these experiences unscathed. At best she finds ways to use the difficult times to grow in strength and in faith. She will learn to deal with men, and other women, as they are, with their hang-ups and attitudes, and not just as women are raised to think of men.

A woman can also end up feeling devastated by some of these experiences in the work world. Yet how threatened do men feel by us if they are called upon

to refer to us in derogatory terms
to isolate us
to make jokes at our expense
to start rumors
to threaten us with physical violence
to make sexual advances

—all of which bring us under their control.

The gradual entry of women into all areas of the workplace appears to be causing a power struggle. Some men apparently consider the workplace their domain. Women can run the home, but a man must run the workplace. To retain control he must have control over the women who enter there.

No one of us needs to have control over another person, but many men, and many women, think they do. As long as this power struggle continues, women will be perceived as a threat in the male-dominated workplace. Women must give up their control over the home and over men; men must give up their control over the workplace. Only through this effort will equality be possible.

We are still a long way from equality. Most women find it difficult to conceive of and deal with men as just persons, like themselves. Women are raised to perceive men as authority figures; as the ones who can do anything; as the ones to do things better than women; as smarter than women; as more skilled than women.

We come in for a rude awakening when confronted by the real person, particularly when this man is the supervisor or a co-worker, and particularly if the work is traditionally that done by men. We women are so used to having low expectations of ourselves in terms of what we can do—but high expectations to achieve perfection—and high expectations of men that the truth is more than we can assimilate. Individual men don't understand all our reactions. How could they? They probably never held themselves up as models of perfection, and never said only men could do what they do. Women often overreact to the reality of the humanness of men by putting men down and ridiculing them.

Perhaps an analogy to race discrimination can help us to understand this noncommunication or comprehension that we as women have of ourselves and of men, and that men have of themselves to some extent and of us.

In the South blacks for generations were treated as second-class citizens. They were allowed to compete with each other, but never with whites. They could succeed as a sharecropper or laborer, and could even become a doctor—to treat other blacks. The colleges that a black could attend could accept only blacks.

Much as the rhetoric within the civil rights movement—long before the movement became popular—said blacks are equal, there were few opportunities for black children to grow up in a way that let them behave as though they were equal to white children. They might believe in equality intellectually, but emotionally they knew where they belonged—within their own society. A black was subservient to a white, had to "bow and shuffle." Even though the black person had ways to manipulate that racist society to retain some identity of self, the black person could not behave as a full member of "white" society.

Few black persons could overcome this burden of believing and behaving as in some way inferior. Within this context the strength of a Rosa Parks to sit in the front of the bus is inspiring. She believed in herself and was able to exercise this belief, to stand up and be counted, alone. She and others became models to other blacks to start to change their behavior to one of equality rather than of subservience.

The catchphrases of "Black is beautiful" and "We shall overcome" have tremendous psychological power, and are necessary to blacks beginning to exercise their status of equality. If you feel inside that you are inferior because you are black (or because you are female), you can never live as a full person, expecting to be treated as an equal *and* treating others as equals.

Racism is far from eradicated from this society, but in some ways we are farther ahead in identifying racism than in recognizing and addressing sexism. The white and black societies, especially in the South, certainly are easier to see and examine than are the male and female societies within both the black and white communities. As with racism, it is mainly women who are trying to understand the male and female societies and to bring themselves from a subservient role to one of equality. But when you are part of the problem—in this case when you bear the traits of subservience and oppression—analyzing and changing those traits, and the society, are all the more difficult. Still, it would not be right for us not to initiate the change ourselves. And, this is the freedom, the opportunity, the challenge before us.

I probably shall never forget how extremely difficult it was for me to participate in activities of the women's rights movement which involved confronting male authority figures with their sexism, sexist policies, and sexist practices. By working as a small group we were able to prepare detailed informational analyses which then could be presented in a rational context and solutions proposed. We usually offered to be part of the solution, too, and to do much of the work. Through this method we could deal with the authorities, so long as they responded to the information presented. And, I think, for all of us this was a learning of what a male authority is, a positive experience. We also found that power structures are not some strange phenomenon, and are rather quickly analyzed, and even penetrated.

The emotional level rose when the men would not listen or would not look at the information, but rather refused to discuss or to reveal relevant facts. This happened with a major university, with the result that the university eventually forced the women leaders out and spent at least a million dollars fighting a legal battle. The key complainant in the case died before the case was resolved. But the university has taken some steps to improve the status of women students, faculty, and employees, but they had to do it on their own terms, retaining their power.

Even though in many ways we lost that "battle," as persons we worked through several of our traits of oppression which in turn freed us up to function better in other jobs and situations. Some of these traits of oppression that we tend to exhibit include:

> Accepting the jokes told at our expense so we don't seem oversensitive

Believing the female supervisor is not equal to the male supervisor, and challenging her authority when we would never challenge a man's

Manipulating the male supervisor and sometimes also the male colleague

Competing with other women for attention, with a willingness to put other women down

Feeling a subservience to men and their actions that we do not feel in dealing with women

Not being ourselves around men—supervisors, colleagues—or developing two behavior modes, one in relating to men, one for women

Sensing a belonging with fellow women workers which is not there with male workers, though men seem to have the same belonging among themselves

It is the woman who bears the burden of achieving equality in the workplace, of overcoming these behavior and attitudinal problems. This burden carries with it many components. It means getting men and other women to accept you as a person capable of performing the position you are in, particularly if it is a position normally held by a man (carpenter, driver, electrician, miner, plumber, reporter, doctor, pilot, executive). It means finding ways to relate to co-workers, i.e., the men go to the local bar or the club during or after work; the woman is an outsider. It means being nonthreatening to the male colleagues' wives who resent knowing a woman is associating with their husband at work, or socially in nonwork but work-related situations. It means establishing working conditions under which you can perform well and with confidence. It means establishing communication so that you know what is going on in the workplace, you know what is expected of you, and you can show your own work and results. And it means performing your job without threatening your supervisor or your co-workers.

All in all, it looks as though the woman has to be not just an ordinary human being but some kind of prophet and nonemotional being who can see all and control her responses to produce the appropriate reactions from others in the workplace. The idea of equality is not to make superpersons or nonpersons, so the problem then becomes, how does a woman accomplish these things once she has decided to be a part of the paid work force?

The first step is for the employer and co-workers to share the responsibility for creating a work situation in which the individual woman can be herself and do her job. If the employer and co-workers are unaware of such a responsibility, this has to become the primary task—besides job performance—of the woman employee. She has to create a support network. The biggest mistake women make—and I have made it too many times myself—is to take all the pressure and responsibility on themselves and to convince themselves they can make whatever adjustments are needed to succeed in the job. Or they convince themselves that it doesn't matter that the situation is sexist, telling themselves they can just ignore it and do their own jobs. This approach may work for a while, but it inevitably ends up either as destructive to the woman, so that she can no longer perform her job, or as a confrontation in which the real issues are buried.

The second step is to establish a support group, either within the workplace or outside it (this goes for the woman staying at home, for the volunteer, and for the woman working for pay). This group does not have to become actively involved in any situation or in the workplace, but the group can serve as a sounding board, perhaps adviser, and as support. Sometimes if we can talk through what we are feeling and experiencing, then we can deal with it in a constructive way that benefits all involved.

Women lead an amazingly alone life. When I look to find the supports that I know I need, that we need, I find very few. The neighborhood coffee klatch probably has served this purpose better than anything; yet how many are there now? I didn't realize it at the time, but having women and their children come by for coffee was the greatest pleasure I had when my daughter was still young and mostly at home. We talked and laughed and shared things in a way I have not experienced since I began working regular office hours. Going out for lunch from the office just isn't the same.

With the development of the nuclear family, women became ever more isolated. Men seem always to have managed to establish ways to be together: the male unions and union halls, the male clubs, the male organizations (Kiwanis, Lions), gathering at the local bar. Women don't seem to have anything comparable.

Now that we are moving into jobs which make us isolated even from the traditional woman worker, we are faced with a serious problem—*nowhere* to turn for a support group. We haven't built any over the past couple of centuries, with the exception of various women's auxiliaries and women's clubs. It seems as though we have retreated from the communication, togetherness, sharing that women in the extended family and interdependent smaller community once had. The housewife, the woman executive, the woman miner—all are isolated.

In searching for support groups, what I find first are the work situations in which women do actually work together, and in some cases have formed their own unions—nurses, some office workers, some food service workers. Despite competitiveness the women in these job classes do have a sense of belonging and sharing and helping and supporting each other. Some women have formed community groups or church groups for specific purposes, through which they gain some opportunities for supporting and knowing each other. We have a long way to go to create structures, outside the home, where we feel we belong.

I think churches can be extremely helpful in establishing an effective support network. The church choirs, the Sunday school teaching, the women's auxiliaries, are all places where women tend to gather to enjoy each other's company, to be. These can be expanded to address much more seriously the problem of the isolation of women, in the home, in the workplace, in educational institutions.

These structures to reduce the isolation of women will not come easily. We ourselves resist them. We're afraid of women's clubs and groups, so used are we to all the negative images portrayed of them. We won't go! We won't fit! Some new approaches have to be developed to allow women to get together just to be together, not just to perform a task or service.

Women need not be so alone. We must learn not to expect the impossible from ourselves. We must reach out to each other. We each have feelings and needs, and we have strengths and abilities. Together we can learn to be ourselves, and to have the strength to be ourselves, whether in the home, in the workplace, or as a volunteer.

CHAPTER 4

Woman in the Workplace— Part II

SEXUALITY IN THE WORKPLACE

Women are often perceived quite literally as sex objects, out of and in the workplace. How many offices, construction sites, vehicles have you seen that have pinups decorating the doors and walls of the workplace? Have you ever talked with men working in traditionally male positions who do *not* discuss women mainly as sex objects? Talk with police officers, doctors, truck drivers, printers, male cooks, and others. The language is basically the same; the jokes are the same; the attitude toward women is the same.

Today much of this language is curtailed when a woman is around, but that does not mean the attitude is not there, though it may be expressed in less obvious ways.

It is possible that men hide behind these jokes and attitudes because they find us difficult to deal with. Anytime men can put women in a box, or make us the butt of a joke, they have a sense of power over us. We cannot threaten them if they control us.

But being put in the box is not a good experience. Our sense of being, of freedom, of self-confidence is being denied. If we accept it, we let go some of our personhood. If we challenge it, we begin to fight for our existence, which becomes even more threatening to the men.

Then there is also the willingness of some women to be sex objects, and to be used sexually by men in the workplace. As in decades past, sex is still a way for a woman to gain power, promotions, influence. The woman who provides sexual favors for men in the power hierarchy gains both in power and in status.

In one national organization, secretaries vie for the opportunity to attend the biennial convention, apparently mostly for the change, the travel, and the excitement of seeing people from across the country. The expectation of the men attending that convention, though, I was told, is that the women are there for their sexual pleasure. This is the price paid to be able to attend. One secretary refused to comply with the expectation, which has accordingly hampered her position in the organization, despite her excellent work skills.

Women gossip about each other's sexual activities, and make derogatory remarks about how one woman obtained a promotion over other women. This accusation occurs even when the woman has not participated in any sexual activity in the workplace.

We have to address these realities of sex in the workplace. Our own behavior often is just a sign of our own oppression. To overcome it, we need to bring the pressures, the attitudes, the problems out into the open and deal with them, together. We may never know the extent of the sexual pressures on women in the workplace, or the extent of the work decisions made on the basis of sexuality.

This is not to say that strong loving relationships cannot develop at the workplace. But the woman worker must be aware that if she is approached, she cannot assume the motivation is for friendship or a relationship;

other assumptions about her availability may be being made, or tested.

We are sexual beings. Whether or not this sexuality should be turned off in the workplace is a question for the psychologists. The fact is, though, that at present sex is very much on the minds of many men and women employees. If we are to relate to each other, inevitably some sexuality will be expressed. Whether or not this is a healthy part of communicating and sharing, or whether or not this is use of another person or a means of controlling another person, becomes an important distinction. Once a woman is used sexually by a supervisor or another worker, she is branded and the expectations and competition increase. Her ability to separate job content and sexual performance will decrease proportionately.

As with actual work content, it is important for the woman worker to be aware of her sexuality, her sexual drives and communication, and her value of herself and her sexuality. The same is, of course, true for the male worker, but he is less often the victim of someone else's aggression, since men tend to hold the positions of power in the workplace power hierarchy.

SKILL ASPIRATIONS AND TRAINING

Women do have skills and the ability to obtain and exercise skills, despite the emphasis on sexual performance in some workplaces.

As an individual you want to think about whether or not there are skills that you have and want to use or skills that you want to learn and develop. How important are these skills to your personal fulfillment, and to your mental and physical health? What part do these skill aspirations play in your view of yourself and your life goals?

Defining one's skill aspirations is not easy. Integral to the development and use of skills is the way in which they are used, and what that end product means to you as a person. In addition, most of us have a limited view of what skills are possible or available. Despite all the tests and formal career counseling, the teenager, young adult, or older adult has little help in determining her or his skill aspirations, potential, and options. Nevertheless, decisions must be made. Since developing a skill and a career requires perseverance, time, money, and emotional commitment, it is important to select a direction that brings satisfaction and some return on the investment.

A woman can aspire to almost any skill or career. The EEOC has made this exceptionally clear over the years by denying all requests from employers for BFOQs (Bona Fide Occupational Qualifications) which would have allowed the employer to continue to hire only men for certain positions. The task for us, then, is to open our minds to all the possibilities; to gather the information available on the skill, profession, or training; to make contacts with people in that profession or training; to make a realistic assessment of the skills, the work situation, and the costs.

Even while we are making decisions it is important to keep as many doors open as possible all along the way. Despite our societal and educational efforts to make teenagers decide by age fourteen or fifteen what they want to "be" or "do" for the rest of their lives, as people we do not fit into a single direction. Most of us keep changing as we grow, and to grow we must change. What seemed most important at age twenty may no longer be valued at age forty.

Some people select a skill as a teenager that evolves into their lifework; or they may take a job when young that they stay with the rest of their working lives. Other people change jobs and careers throughout their working lives. Especially over the past decade the mid-point career change, or second career, has become more prevalent: for men in the traditional career sense, for women, moving from being a full-time housewife to getting a college degree and working full-time for pay. Others have opted to leave the traditional world of work and try a totally different life-style, such as buying a farm and becoming self-sufficient.

Decisions on skill aspirations need to reflect the total person. Therefore, analyzing skill aspirations and the desire for training has to be our ongoing task, reflecting our life goals. We should remember, too, that skills can be used in all areas of life. They need not be limited to the workplace.

Volunteer work has provided women with a gold mine for development. The options are enormous, and sometimes the experience is more rewarding than that found in a job for pay. One problem that women sometimes encounter in pursuing their aspirations in the world of work is the frustration over not obtaining the same fulfillment when working for pay that they experience in volunteer work.

Once having set a direction for skill development, we are faced with determining how best to obtain those skills. During the past ten years, for the first time, engineering, law, medical, dental schools have begun to open their doors to women students in large numbers. Women are no longer automatically channeled into nursing, teaching, arts, and humanities courses. Government-backed affirmative action requirements have been responsible for most of this opening up of opportunities for women to obtain education and training in the professions.

Training in the trades similarly is gradually opening up to women, again in response to government action. In April 1978 the U.S. Department of Labor issued to construction contractors who were utilizing government funds the goals of employing women for 3.1 percent of their work force by April 1979, and for 6.9 percent by April 1981. This action followed an analysis of women apprentices registered in all construction trades which showed that women represented only 2.3 percent, despite an increase of 38 percent between 1976 and 1977.

In May 1978 the Department of Labor issued regulations calling for one fifth of entering apprentices to be women in the first year, with an increase to occur each year thereafter. The Department of Labor also suggested that employers should take some responsibility in notifying women of apprenticeship opportunities and should initiate programs to prepare and encourage women to enter traditionally male programs.

Data on the impact of the regulations and on the attainment of the goals are not available.

With major cutbacks in manufacturing jobs and in government training funds, training in the trades is becoming more restricted, though the doors have been opened.

Cutbacks in government funds for education have had a serious impact on women. Since women are predominantly in the lower paid service type of positions, they do not have the money to continue their education and so be able to move into more skilled positions. If women come from families headed by women, they usually do not have family financial support for training and education, and they have fewer options traditionally than do men of obtaining employment that encourages training and education.

Given the increase in professional jobs, and the relatively more open policy of professional schools, women can reasonably consider entering almost any profession. Obtaining an apprenticeship is measurably more difficult, and the end goal of obtaining a job not as promising.

However, women can also consider private entrepreneurship—starting their own business using their own skills.

Women have been running their own informal businesses for centuries: they take in sewing, they baby-sit, they clean houses, they cook and bake, they tutor, they do laundry. Many a woman has raised a family from the income gained through these efforts. Today we find more women opening shops that sell arts and crafts, baked goods, secondhand articles; clothing boutiques; and beauty salons. There are myriads of possibilities, limited only by our imaginations and by what others will spend money to buy.

Many of us still just go out and get a job, any job, rather than think about work as a vital part of our lives that needs to be planned through a course of education and training. Why we do this is not clear, though the reasons probably are a mix of psychological barriers, financial limitations, lack of confidence, and exterior barriers in schools and training programs. The options and the opportunities are unlimited, but it is up to us to seek them out, and to pursue them.

YOUR HEALTH AND THE WORKPLACE

What makes you feel good, physically and mentally? Do you ever think about this? Are you physically fit? Do you pay attention to what you put into your body—food, beverage, pills, drugs? Do you pay attention to stressful situations, to pressures that you, or others, put you under?

The work environment directly relates to a person's mental and physical health. Some general interrelationships include:

Consumption of alcohol. In many work situations the drink at lunch or after work is part of the social exchange among workers; the person who does not drink is different and may end up being excluded from these gatherings; it is not unusual for major work decisions to be made "over drinks."

Consumption of food. Three meals a day is often too much food for the body to use, especially if the body gets minimal physical activity; lunch on the job is *the* social occasion of the day; for many managers and workers, meeting people for breakfast and also for lunch—sometimes for dinner too—is the way the day becomes bearable. In addition, social occasions with the boss or with co-workers also usually involve food and drink.

Consumption of cigarettes and coffee. These serve as a partial alternative to consumption of alcohol, and are part of nearly all work and social exchanges: the women's coffee klatch, the morning and afternoon coffee break at work, coffee at meetings, cigarettes to relieve tension.

Sedentary life and work patterns. The most physical activity most adults get is in taking care of the home; few of us have a regular exercise program or goals; most of us ride to work, ride to the store, ride to school; we have all kinds of mechanical assists, at home and at work. As technological changes are put in place the number of jobs requiring any physical labor becomes less and less. Now robots are becoming more popular. Most of us sit or stand in one place all day. This sedentary pattern ensures that we also have no way to work out tensions, frustrations, or stress. The exhaustion we feel at the end of the day is not physical. In fact, with some exercise we find we are not tired at all.

Anxiety and stress. Once the goal of making money and buying material things has become as pervasive as it now is in our society, and with the more sedentary work requirements, anxiety and stress emerge as rather consistent forces in all of us. The stress of work demands has no release, and so the anxiety and pressure end up causing ulcers, heart attacks and high blood pressure, mental illness, dysfunction in various parts of our bodies and our lives.

From the way many of us go to the doctor (and women go more frequently than men), it would seem we do care about our health. We know we cannot function successfully when we don't feel well. But we need only look around us—and perhaps at ourselves—to find the majority of people doing things in their daily lives that are destructive to their health, because other values have taken precedence. The alcohol, food, cigarette, and coffee consumption described so briefly above often seems necessary to success on the job.

We are beginning to see a change in this. More and more executives are taking count of their health. Stroke and heart attack victim statistics have begun to sink in, and personal health concerns are rising to priority status. Anxiety, stress, and exercise programs are all now being talked about. Several urban YWCAs and YMCAs provide exercise facilities for workers during lunch breaks and right after work. Women have an easier time creating options for themselves around food, drink, and exercise than do men, since women are supposed to be concerned about their figures and looks. Men don't want a fat or alcoholic female in the office.

Some stress is healthy, and constructive. But women sometimes are subjected to negative behaviors that create a destructive stress and anxiety. In a 1975 study the

National Institute on Occupational Hazards found women secretaries particularly subject to stress. Some of the practices that tend to produce this stress for women in the workplace are:

> the sexual jokes using women as the victim
>
> the sexual passes by supervisors, co-workers, and workers being supervised
>
> the put-downs of the male supervisor threatened by a competent woman employee
>
> the rumors
>
> the testing of a woman's endurance
>
> the manipulative roles we develop in situations in which we have not been treated as equals
>
> the lack of a support network resulting in psychological isolation
>
> never being a member of the "boys" club, and/or losing our identity in trying to become "one of the guys"
>
> the competition among women for male attention

All of us, male and female, want and need to be allowed to do a good job; to be respected and treated with dignity; to receive support and encouragement; to know what is expected and to be given the opportunity to fulfill the expectations. A work situation that does not provide these components is probably unhealthy for any worker. The pressures that can exist, that can be created, in the workplace can cause the worker to become ill, both physically and mentally.

A woman entering a nontraditional job is likely to face more unhealthy working conditions than the woman in a more traditional position. It is critical that she take steps to improve the conditions, to alleviate the stress and anxiety, and to protect her own mental and physical health. Building the support network is essential.

While employers are becoming more aware of the costs to themselves of unhealthy working environments, few have seriously addressed the effects of discrimination on an employee's work productivity or on the employee's physical or mental health. Despite the fact that a major portion of an employer's costs involve personnel, most employers do not pay attention to unhealthy work environments and conditions.

We need to place a high value on our personal health. Without good health we severely, and unnecessarily, limit our options and life goals. Looking after our health is our personal responsibility.

OPTIONS

We have the opportunity to head in a variety of directions for our work. All careers are open to us. We have a myriad of volunteer opportunities available as organizations come to place a much higher value on their volunteer workers. And, being a wife, a mother, a homemaker is still open to us, as is any combination of the three.

In considering our options we need to examine at some length work situations, skill and training opportunities, job content, working conditions, our personal values, opportunity for self-fulfillment, our coping skills, and our financial needs and wants. The key is to know ourselves. Then we must discipline ourselves to analyze the situation into which we intend to place ourselves.

Most of us just fall into things. A choice of career is likely to result from liking a particular teacher or professor, or being in a school where the courses in this area are interesting, or having a role model, or needing a job and taking whatever comes first. With all the technical assists, decision-making always comes back to us. What information we gather and examine depends on our own vision. Our selection, our awareness of options, is based on our knowledge of ourselves, our self-confidence, and our ability to look beyond the immediate. We can, in fact, create our options. Surely there are ways and means yet untried. Let us gather our energies and our imagination and go to it. We may fail—once, twice, three times—but never, really, for we learn and grow from everything we try. Throughout we simply must respond to our inner selves, to our vocation.

SOME QUESTIONS TO CONSIDER

PRODUCTIVITY AND VOCATIONAL/JOB DECISIONS

1. What are the characteristics of a job that I need to be productive?

>Do I need variety?
>
>Do I need to be in one place, or moving about?
>
>Do I need contact and communication with fellow workers?
>
>Do I need contact and communication with people outside the workplace?
>
>Do I need to be relatively independent in performing work assignments?
>
>Do I need a supportive supervisor?
>
>Do I need private, and/or quiet, work space, or do I need to have people around?

2. What do I need to motivate me to work hard and well?

>Do I need to be challenged intellectually and/or in use of skills?
>
>Do I need to believe that what I am doing is useful?

Do I need to believe that I am helping other people to do their own jobs, to be happier or healthier, to live more comfortably?

Do I need satisfaction from my work to be able to continue?

Do I like routine?

Do I thrive on problem-solving, or would I rather not be faced with problems?

Do I need clearly defined and limited tasks, or do I need the freedom and authority to work out the tasks?

3. What do I find satisfying about working?

Is the amount of salary critical?

Do I need to have a finished product to show for my time and effort?

Do I like being a cog that makes a wheel run more smoothly and efficiently?

Do I need to be told by fellow workers, supervisor, outsiders that I am doing a good job?

Do I need to be able to see some effect or change as the result of my work?

Do I need people to know and appreciate what I put into my work?

Areas to be examined when considering a specific work situation or position include:

Knowing who your supervisor will be and assessing your ability to communicate and work with her or him. Supervisors can and do change, but the initial assessment is important, nevertheless.

Knowing your fellow workers and assessing their attitudes toward each other and toward their work, and taking a look at their morale

Location and type of work space. Can you function in it?

Job content. Are you clear about what you will be doing? About your responsibilities? How will you get your job assignments, and from whom? Can you be self-directed? To what extent?

Opportunities for advancement. Are there any women in supervisory or management positions? What proportion? Where are they? Is there an affirmative action plan with goals that ensure opportunities for you?

Benefits and pay scales. Are they what you want and need? Are women paid equally to men? How is pay established? Is there one benefit package for all employees? Can you have flexible hours?

"Vibes"—take these seriously. How does the workplace feel to you? Are women the butt of office jokes? How do employees dress? Does this fit with your own sense of work dress? Will you be comfortable?

Extracurricular commitments. Are there any? Will you be expected to entertain? Are you to go to dinner with the boss? Are there weekend seminars where you will be the only woman? Do you sense any other pressures for your time or personal involvement?

HEALTH AND VOCATIONAL/JOB DECISIONS

1. Do I have any chronic health conditions to take into account? List:
   Condition
   Environmental requirements
   Care/maintenance requirements
   Time/money requirements

   What considerations do I need to make in choosing a job or other vocational commitment?

2. What health costs do I have that either I must be able to pay for or I need to have covered by employer-paid insurance?

> Physical health care
> Eye care
> Ear care
> Dental care
> Mental health care
> Summarize health care costs for the past year, including prescriptions.
> List health insurance coverage and annual premium and whether or not each is paid by the employer or by you.

3. What makes me feel good, mentally and physically?
4. What situations tend to make me feel bad, mentally and/or physically?
5. What conditions do I need in a work environment to feel healthy and energetic?

EMOTIONAL NEEDS
AND VOCATIONAL/JOB DECISIONS

1. Do I have emotional needs that must be satisfied through my job?

> being wanted or needed?
> having a place to be within a defined structure?
> using my creative energies?
> meeting and communicating with people?
> being with people?
> providing help to people?
> feeling productive?
> having some status and position?

2. Do I have a fulfilling life outside the workplace, or is this my main source of exchange with people?

> Who are my closest friends? Where did I meet them? How do I maintain the friendship?

Who are my family's friends? How does the family maintain the friendship?

What time do I spend outside the workplace with friends?

What time do I spend with friends made at work?

Do I arrange this time, or do I leave the initiative to others?

What do I look for in a friendship?

3. Do I need to work in a supportive environment? Do I need my superiors to pay attention to and care about my work?

4. Do I need feedback on my work?
   from my supervisor
   from colleagues
   from outsiders

5. Do I need some control over my environment and my work?

6. Do I need to have authority over others, or do I prefer not to have authority or to supervise?

7. What do I need to motivate me to work at capacity?

PERSONAL VALUES

1. Why do I work, or want to work? List in order of priority:
   money
   status
   authority and power
   satisfaction
   use skills
   be independent and self-sufficient
   help others
   be productive

avoid being home alone
learn and develop skills
feel wanted and needed

2. What material things do I need and/or want?

Need   *Want*

a home
a car
health, eye, dental care
car, home, health insurance
food and clothing
furniture
appliances
vacation
education
hobby
eating out
leisure activities (specify)

3. What am I looking for in a job? Check those which are important.
financial security
benefits that give me health care security
satisfaction of using skills and abilities
meeting new people
having the opportunity to try new things
satisfaction of doing something that helps others, directly or indirectly
productive use of my time

4. What values must I be able to express? Check those which are important.
honesty
respect for myself and others
having others be fair with me
open two-way communication with colleagues and supervisors

behaving in a responsible manner
keeping mind and body healthy
helping other people, and receiving help from
   them
treating people with dignity
having respect for my work and the work of others

CHAPTER 5

Interpersonal Relationships, Family, and Home

SEXUALITY

As Christian theology has evolved, the family has become the model structure for our personal life. The Roman Catholic Church raises the holy family and Mary, as mother of God, almost to a position of worship. The belief in the virgin birth and the Immaculate Conception further heightens woman as mother, and lessens the role of the father in the family. Statues, paintings, and carvings in churches often portray the mother and child; hardly ever the father and child. There is a clear message here—to women and to men. The narrow view of women presented by a number of churches is limiting to the woman seeking her vocation, the full spectrum of options for her life, her mission.

What the churches present is not necessarily the essence of Christianity or of Christian belief. Feminist theologians suggest otherwise. It certainly is possible to interpret the Bible in ways that allow a woman to develop into full personhood, equal to that of a man, and not necessarily very different.

Protestants on the whole have reflected the emphasis on family somewhat differently from the Roman Catholic

Church, but the place for the wife and mother is usually depicted as being in the home, taking care of things related to the family. The economic changes at the time of the Reformation made it possible for the male head of the household to begin to leave the home to work, and to bring money home to buy what was needed. Many women still did piecework, but often in the home. Gradually they, too, had to leave the home to work in the factories, but the goal was still for the woman to be in the home, and for the better off family, for her to be looked after.

Though mythical, this still is thought to be the norm for the American family. If a person is not happily part of a full family, then that person in some way is considered not quite to belong to this society. The reality is that there are not very many "whole and happy" families in this mythological sense: many parents are divorced; many women, and some men, are single; many children are born out of wedlock; many adults are alcoholics, are drug abusers, are child abusers, are mentally disturbed; so many families find that blood kinship does not bring love and belonging.

Just as we need to broaden our definition and perception of vocation, so do we need to broaden our view of the family. We don't have to feel the pressure to create and retain the nuclear family. It is more important that we be, that we follow what is right for us, what we understand as God's will.

The Roman Catholic Church seems to be particularly concerned about our sexuality. Intertwined with the pressure to marry and have a family are prohibitions on birth control and abortion, and a general opposition to sex education. Both priests and nuns are to be celibate, and their lives are considered of a higher state in dedication to God.

This preoccupation with the sexuality of women is worth noting, for it has affected our attitudes toward our own sexuality. There is some guilt. There is some sense of inferiority, of being victimized. The amounts of money spent to oppose birth control, abortion, and planned parenthood are immense. I suspect far more is spent in this opposition, and certainly the emotional content is higher, than is spent to help mothers raise their children or is spent on making certain young children have enough to eat. When Congress cut funds for school meal programs, the outcry from Catholic organizations was less than a whisper as compared to their opposition to abortion.

Indeed we are sexual beings, as are men. What we do with our sexuality, though, has more lasting effects on our lives and our options than is the case for men. Therefore, concern with our sexual behavior is critical to our own freedom and well-being. This ultimately means deciding whether or not to have one or more children. Many of us who have children never made this a conscious decision. It is just that one should have children. This lack of decision-making has been difficult at times even for the children. Our goal, whether thought out or not, was to have children. This may or may not have been a true goal or vocation in the broader sense.

Since women are held responsible for the children, we women must exercise control over our sexual lives. We need to work through how we relate to men, what they expect from us, what we expect from them. We are a long way from this.

Since there is no sex education in most schools, families, or churches, and minimal birth control information, the female teenager all too often ends up becoming pregnant long before she is ready to make any lifetime decisions. Teenagers today are sexually active. Though their parents might not agree with their behavior, the reality is that the majority of boys and girls graduating from high school have been involved sexually with a person of the opposite sex. More and more are having "unwanted teenage pregnancies."

We have not given teenage girls or boys the information to make it possible for them to be responsible in their actions. It is not so long ago that most people married in their mid and late teens, so sexual activity for teenagers is not new. It is just that our life patterns have changed.

How a young person, or an older person, is to go about learning about her or his sexuality and needs is a difficult question. We are pretty much left to what we can read, learn from others, or gain from experience, which could be positive, or negative. This is not the way we want our children to learn about other, less emotional, and perhaps less important, subjects. And it is not the way we go about learning about a new subject. Sexuality is such a charged subject some of us never deal with it.

Theologically sex is presented as an integral part of marriage, a way of sharing love and fulfilling the union of man and woman. This image does convey a recognition of our being, but it doesn't take us far enough to give us the self-understanding and direction we need in setting life goals and making decisions. Planning out one's total life within the Christian framework and tradition is new for most women. The path is not well worn.

FAMILY COMMITMENTS AND RELATIONSHIPS

The commitments we make to other people are usually directly related to our own needs at the time. Those commitments involve self-discipline for meeting others' needs as well, and usually over a long period of time. These lasting bonds require a conscious working out of responsibilities and functions.

If we take family and homemaking as an example, there are certain things that must be taken care of:

> Each family member needs clothing, which must be bought or made, laundered, kept in a defined space accessible to that person.
>
> Each family member needs a place for cleaning her or his person, normally a bathroom with tub and/or shower, and this must be kept clean and in repair.
>
> The garbage must be disposed of.
>
> The living space of each family member, and of the whole family, must be kept clean and in repair.
>
> The children need places to play, a stimulating environment, and places for their own things.
>
> Each family member needs space for sleeping, living.
>
> Everyone needs to eat properly and regularly, which entails shopping, cooking, serving, cleaning up, and money to buy and prepare the food.
>
> The family members need time together and time apart.
>
> Each family member has emotional needs that must be met.
>
> Adults need places to relax, to keep hobbies, to do what is satisfying to them, just to be.
>
> And so on . . .

The women's movement encourages a sharing of these responsibilities by all family members. When children are involved, at certain ages there are things they cannot do, but from age two and up, there are things they can do. Adults may do one thing better than another, but even that does not mean adults should not teach each other to do everything, and periodically shift the tasks. If there is only one adult, some provision has to be made to get everything done, which sometimes means having money to hire a skilled person.

Time often becomes the most critical issue or concern in interpersonal and family relationships and commitments. Time, therefore, must also be a key question in deciding our work, in seeking our vocation, and in making a decision on a particular task or job.

We all know any number of wives and husbands who are critical of their spouse's use of time. The husband is accused of working such long hours he is never home; or, when he isn't working he is off with the boys or out on the golf course. The wife may spend too many hours at work, or she is off doing some volunteer thing when she should be at home cooking dinner so it will be ready when husband and children want to eat. Or, perhaps, the husband never takes time to be with the children, or to do any work around the house. He just comes home and sits in front of the television, or with his nose in a newspaper.

Some families deal with these problems by scheduling times and activities for the family as a whole, for the parents, or for the children. Scheduling performance of household chores also helps take the pressure off, if the person can accept the discipline of a household schedule. Without a schedule someone usually ends up having to nag, and then tensions build and problems arise.

Being married and having children, not being married and having children, or having a relationship involve some major commitments of time and of one's self to other people. Both men and women need to recognize this commitment and to be prepared to give whatever is required to make the relationship or marriage work, to keep the family functioning. This commitment cannot be just in earning money, but needs to involve a sharing of one's own self.

The woman working in the home and the man working outside the home is not the best division of labor. For the man to have a commitment to home and family, he must be an integral part of both, and this means he must be involved in keeping the home and in raising the family. The woman should never take on all these functions, and thereby exclude the man. Likewise, the woman needs to have interests outside the home. Too much inner concentration and isolation can create tensions and problems which otherwise would not exist, including the potential of trying to live her life through her husband and children.

If the man is going to take on some of the functions of running the home, the woman needs to look at how she can help in sustaining the family. This might be through doing community and volunteer work, or it might be to earn money. If the family needs money to meet the basic needs for survival, then she has to find work for pay. The solution is not for the man to take a second job, be home even less, and thereby be further excluded from his home and family.

Neither parent should control the home or the family. Sharing eliminates power struggles. Each family member needs nurturing and support to grow and to fulfill his or her vocation.

All parents must consider how much time their "work" keeps them away from home. They need to consider what emotional and psychological state they are in when they do come home. Is the job frustrating or depressing? Does it require large amounts of travel, or of work even at home? Does the job entail social engagements and entertainment? How do these affect the family, and the finances?

Then there are the responsibilities of the extended family. Are the parents and relatives in good health? Do any need supportive care, or money to get help in their home? Do any live with the immediate family? What are their needs?

All these factors and values interrelate in any work decision-making, but they must be considered by every person involved. If a woman and a man decide to marry and to have children, they must also decide to make time, energy, and value commitments to each other and to the children. Fulfillment of this commitment, morally and theologically, must come at the top of every list of choices and possible directions. This doesn't mean that you ignore your own needs; it simply means that you do not ignore those persons with whom you have established interdependencies, and with children, dependencies. There are circumstances and situations that an individual is forced to leave, sometimes to salvage one's own self. Even in extreme situations, though, we must still strive to carry out responsibilities taken on by choice.

Decisions about marriage and family are similar in practice to decisions about work and career. Today most are made without much thought or consideration of their implications, costs, or potential. When we are young and in love, getting married seems the obvious thing to do. What else is there to consider? And having chidren? Of course. This without thought to what it entails, whether or not there is money, whether or not either parent or both parents are ready. Just as we know little about sex until we "try" it, so we seem to know little about marriage and children and families. This is not to say we have to become rational about everything, just more aware, thoughtful, and, yes, prayerful. We need to be attuned to our vocation.

Some churches have taken steps to help young people entering marriage, but even here they reach only those who make wedding plans in advance, and so have started down the path of planning and decision-making. It would be good if churches could make classes available to persons at all stages of marriage and child-rearing.

This might provide the support and guidance that so many married couples, single parents, and single persons seek, yet cannot find.

We do have a strange phenomenon in our society: one is a child until age eighteen, and then magically becomes an adult. As a child one cannot receive sex education; as an adult one is already to have been educated. Churches have Sunday school classes for children; fewer for teenagers; and almost none for adults. It is almost as though once one reaches eighteen or twenty-one, one is to stop learning, growing, or changing. We see this in general education, too. Lifetime decisions are made, and then life is over. We are supposed to settle into a permanent routine with permanent unchanging relationships.

We all know this is not real, and especially not in today's world of intense and rapid change in everything around us. But how many people do you know who seriously try to live as though it is true? They have to die to themselves, to each other, to those around them, to those they could be reaching out to.

Marriage, truly, is a beginning. For a healthy relationship to continue, both members have to grow and change, and so does the relationship. Sometimes people do grow away from each other, but with good communication and sharing usually they can grow as part of a whole. Within our present economic and social structures often it is the woman who goes through the more radical changes and so creates some crises in the relationship. If the relationship is to survive, both partners have to be well attuned to themselves, as well as to each other.

I have a friend who is married and has two children. She feels estranged from her husband, and now that he is unemployed and at home with the children, also from the children. She works long hours, perhaps just to be out of the house, and recently she began drinking heavily.

We talk in bits once in a while, and it seems clear that she expects herself to be able to handle anything, and to get through any problems. She isn't willing, or able, to accept help. One day I asked her why she didn't leave since she seemed in such pain. She replied: "I couldn't do that to him. He wouldn't understand." She went on to explain how she had always just said "yes" to whatever, even though she may have gone ahead and done as she intended. Now she can't play that game anymore, and he hasn't been able to hear her when she tries to explain. Neither parent is able to cope.

Women are still awakening to themselves and to opportunities that heretofore were not open to them. Work for women generally has been perceived as the work in the home and in the community. If the woman also worked outside the home for pay, that tended to be the secondary responsibility, with the purpose being to earn enough money to survive. For the man, the reverse has been true, at least in terms of time commitments. This is reflected in the attitudes of employers toward women as well as in many women's attitudes toward their jobs. It is also reflected in the pay status of women as compared to that of men. We expect the man to work. The woman has a choice, though in reality she may not. Perhaps a better way to look at these attitudes would be to say that, for the woman, the job is a means to an end; for the man, the job is an end in itself. None of this is to say that the woman does not take her job seriously, or work very hard, or deserve equal pay, career opportunities, and all the rest.

The revolution for men may be coming, when the male causes the crisis in the marriage and the home by wanting to leave his job and work in the home, or to take a less demanding, or part-time, job to allow him more time for himself and those close to him. Relationships between men and women are going through radical changes. Women, in particular, are expecting something from the marriage; men may well also begin to look at the emotional and personal content and quality of the marriage.

In a gross sort of way marriage has taken on the characteristics of a contract for keeping house, raising children, doing the washing and ironing, preparing the meals—for the woman; for bringing home enough money to buy housing, food, clothing—for the man. Many spouses have no other communication, except for periodic physical sexual contact, which may or may not include emotional communication and satisfaction.

In this section on family commitments and relationships we need to concern ourselves, too, with the individual woman trying to lose herself in the family, to become totally dependent. The healthy family nurtures the development and growth of each family member. For the children this seems clear. But even there we must be careful of making assumptions.

Think about some families you know, even your own father and mother. Were you allowed—were you encouraged—to grow, to become independent? Or, did your mother need you to remain dependent on her? Did or does she need to cook for you? to do your laundry? to clean your room?

What did your mother do with her time once you went away for part of the day to school and then became involved in activities outside the home, and then moved away from home? What need did she fulfill through you when you were young? as you grew older?

How are you with your own children? Are you a support, a vehicle for them to grow into free individual persons? Or are you the gate that shuts them in, preventing them from trying their wings?

Perhaps because men are more "of the world" than women, they tend to be the adult with whom the older child identifies, which sometimes lends to the mother increasing, rather than decreasing, her dependencies and demands on the child. Although every family member can and should expect some nurturing from other family members, each must also have other friends, activities, challenges, and means of being fulfilled. What these are depends on the situation and the individual.

For many women the family consumes the entirety of their vocational goals. This is the more traditional role expected of women, but it too must be examined as a valid life commitment. Not that a woman is "just a housewife," but that she is seeking her fulfillment as a person through the home, family, and community, perhaps through care of relatives or neighbors.

It is difficult in this society for such a woman to achieve a sense of well-being, of equality, and of accomplishment. It is also extremely difficult for the father-husband to have full involvement with the home and family, for this has to be her bailiwick. She needs to have the children look to her; and she may need them to be dependent on her. She needs to have most, if not all, of the household chores, so she has the satisfaction of making the home run smoothly. She must ensure that she is needed for the well-being of the home and family; and then the husband/father must rely on his work to fulfill his need to be needed.

The chances of success in fulfilling personal needs is usually greater when there is a mix of goals, dependencies, and responsibilities. The workplace may not be the place to try to fulfill one's emotional needs. The home may not be the place to try to fulfill one's needs for status and power.

Knowledge of ourselves, of our needs, of our goals again becomes critical in making decisions, this time relating to family, home, and interpersonal relationships. We are all different, and the maximum number of options needs to be available to each of us as we function on our own and in concert with others. But we must be careful; and we must be somewhat hard with ourselves in observing our needs and how we fulfill them, so that we don't walk into our own traps which end up being destructive to ourselves and to those around us.

We all need family, or persons close to us. Therefore, we must make our decisions in conjunction with those persons. Work should not exclude family; and family should not exclude work. Money, status, respect, self-worth are necessary to healthy relationships and to survival in our society and economy. The family will be stronger and healthier when all members seek total vocation, and total fulfillment.

SHOULD I HAVE CHILDREN?

Should this question be asked and answered only by women? One of the most meaningful outcomes of the women's movement has been an emerging understanding that the father of a child is truly a parent. As parent he has an important role to play in raising and caring for the child. Women are having to let go some of the control they have historically exercised over the home and children; but men need still to pick up more of the responsibility, extended far beyond the provision of money.

Although such an understanding is emerging, few men are prepared—and fewer employers are prepared to accept such men—actually to carry out the time commitments required in being involved in running a home and raising children. Do you remember the film *Kramer vs. Kramer* in which Dustin Hoffman played the single male parent trying to continue a career and raise a son? The employer couldn't accept the father's involvement with his son. That same employer might have accepted similar family involvement on the part of a woman employee, but as a result would never consider her for the responsible position held by Hoffman.

Employers still expect twenty-four-hour commitment for high paid jobs. Having to go home to look after children, cook dinner, be with one's spouse is not high on the value list for most employers. They do seek male managers who have settled home lives, and wives who will entertain, but they look for wives who will not make demands on the man for his time or attention; who will support his "career," and the company.

For some women, some men, some marriages, such an arrangement may work. For many it doesn't. If your husband has such a position, with such demands on him—and you, do not plan to have children unless you are prepared to carry 100 percent of the responsibility for the home and the children, with him being there when he can.

Having children and counting on community resources and services to help with their care and upbringing is not a very safe choice. Some employers do make provisions for child care. But in a study conducted by the Women's Bureau of the U.S. Department of Labor, the researchers found a decrease in hospital-sponsored centers of 23 percent between 1968 and 1978. In conducting a broader survey in 1978 of employer-sponsored child care centers, the bureau found a total of 105 civilian centers that enrolled 8,419 children; and 200 centers located at military installations that served 25,059 children. A woman, or a family, therefore, cannot reasonably expect to find employer-sponsored day care. Part of the reason for the decrease was that the employers found the centers were not used enough, i.e., they did not collect enough money in fees to meet the costs. Other child care facilities are available, but their cost, hours, and care vary tremendously from locale to locale.

So much of our social and economic structure depends on the woman, or someone, being at home, or being free to be at home, that it is difficult to have children if you do not have this flexibility. This situation in no way reflects the realities of our social and economic situation, and it produces painful conflicts and guilt within women, men, marriages, and families. We should still ask: Why shouldn't I or we be able both to have children and to earn a living? even to have the flexibility to move in and out of the work force?

A couple who is deciding whether or not to have children needs to address the following questions:

> What will be the additional cost? Is there money to meet this cost, with one parent or both parents working?
>
> If the woman is working, can the family get along without her paycheck for some period of time (depending on the plans, and allowing for health emergencies)?
>
> How will the child be cared for while either parent or both parents are working?
>
> What adjustments need to be made in household chores?
>
> Who will get up at night (or can this be shared)?
>
> Who will stay home when a child is sick, or is there a neighbor or relative to come in?
>
> Who will arrange for baby-sitters and child care, and transportation?
>
> Who will pay for baby-sitters and child care? for what?
>
> Who will go to community events with the child?
>
> Who will listen when the child needs someone to talk to, or when the caregiver needs to complain, or has a problem to resolve?
>
> Who will take the child to the doctor and dentist?

Who will help with the child's schoolwork?

Who will make sure the child gets off to school and gets home safely?

Who will prepare the family budget, and pay the bills?

Who will handle car pooling to take children here and there?

Millions of families have coped with all these questions, and more, and all the family members have survived, even thrived. It is possible to have children and to work outside the home. It just takes a good deal of organizing, planning, sharing, and working together. One aspect of a family sharing in a multitude of responsibilities is the learning gained by the child in self-care and responsibility. There is no better preparation for independence, freedom, and adulthood.

Family and interpersonal relationships are in some way a part of every person's life, and they become part of every person's vocation. We all seek happiness and fulfillment as persons. I believe this is possible to achieve, perhaps even more possible now that both women and men have so many more options open to them—in their work and careers and in their personal lives. The removal of many of the traditional restrictions opens up opportunities. But change comes slowly, and painfully. Still the concept of vocation covering our entire lives necessitates involvement of the whole person. Vocation requires one to be responsive not only to oneself but to those around, and to God. This wholeness can produce a happiness, a love, a peace, a beauty—though sometimes fleeting—that brings new life.

SOME QUESTIONS TO CONSIDER

FAMILY COMMITMENTS AND RESPONSIBILITIES

1. What are my home and family responsibilities? (List)
   chores
   number of children and care required
   other relatives needing care or assistance
   shopping
   doing things together
2. What are my community involvements with family, children, friends? (List)
   church
   scouting
   neighborhood groups
   music and dance lessons
   athletics
   other
3. What are the emotional needs of my spouse or partner, my children? What role do I play in meeting these needs?
4. What emotional needs do I have that are filled by my spouse or partner, my children?
5. To what extent is the family, or are other persons, dependent on me to earn money to pay living costs?

HOW DO I USE MY TIME?

Time-planning and management have to be considered in making any vocational, and family, decisions. Time allotments don't have to be rigid, but commitments usually require a regular consumption of time.

Responsibility/Activity/Function	*Hours a Week*	*Hours a Month*
chores at home (List)		
shopping		
care of children		
family time		
time with friends		
meals		
sleep		
hobbies		
leisure/social activities		
exercise or recreation		
travel to and from work		
work outside the home		
for pay		
as a volunteer		
paying bills; keeping financial records		
other home and family business (insurance, car maintenance, home repairs, etc.)		
other (List)		

CHAPTER 6

Money

Money necessarily plays a critical role in all vocational and family decision-making. Money is essential to survival. How one obtains and uses money reflects our personal values, life goals, and vocation.

Money is the means to buy what we need and what we want. If we have a supply of money, we have a certain independence and freedom in a way we do not have without money. Many women have no money which they control. If they do not work for pay, and if their spouse does not give them any financial control, they live on an allowance, much as they may have had as children. They ask for whatever money they get, sometimes down to specifics such as money to buy a pair of shoes for a child.

Many women easily give up any access to or control over the money of the household. They never write checks. They never participate in decisions about how to handle the money. No major purchases—home, car, money certificates—are in their name. If anything happens to the marriage, or to the spouse, they are left dysfunctional in a world of buying and selling. They have no idea what to do, where to start, what they need, what they do not need for insurance, investments, taxes. They are at the mercy of whoever decides to "help" them.

Unless one is taking the vow of poverty and following an ascetic life, access to and control over money is necessary to well-being, to freedom, and to independence, in and out of marriage. Women have yet to learn to be comfortable with, and knowledgeable about, money in the way that men are. We have all been affected by the myths that women don't know anything about money and can't learn; and that money is dirty. All these myths do is leave all the power and control to men. This is not equality; and it is not healthy for a relationship. Money cannot be separated totally from love, from family, from running a home. In a very real sense in our society money *is* power.

Women, as well as men, work for money, for money brings control, status, a measure of self-worth and security, and respect. Without money all of these are hard to come by. The issue for women should not be whether or not we need money, just as that is not the issue for men. If our economy is ever changed to more equalization and sharing of wealth, then the question of need can be applied to everyone. But for the present, need is not a measure for men, is not a measure for doctors and lawyers and company presidents, so it should not be a measure for women.

Money is power and influence. Therefore, money should be equally available to women and to men, in the family and in the workplace. You undoubtedly wondered, back when I mentioned money as being a major reason for women to work for pay, just at what point money is needed and at what point money is wanted. Every individual will ultimately have to decide the importance of money and material belongings in her or his life. We have very mixed guidance on these questions in Western society, and in Christianity.

The ascetic saints suggest that being without material wealth is healthy for the soul. One should not have much to eat, and no fancy houses or servants, no signs of wealth. Our lives should be kept simple and directly open to God. Priests, monks, and nuns all take a vow of poverty. They limit their personal ownership, but many are well provided for by the church, carrying all the trappings of wealth. Still their own lives are kept simple and unencumbered by not being involved in home ownership or immediate family.

However, the offices of the church reflect power, status, and wealth. The poor were tithed to build the large cathedrals, and even the small community churches in this country. Tithes also pay for the richness in some church structures and functions today.

Similarly, as the Reformation brought new emphasis to the nuclear family in an industrialized economy, the chosen people became those with wealth and resultant power. The middle-class male who achieved success as a merchant or businessman became admired as God's elect and rose to a position of power within the Reformation churches. Church boards and councils took on the decision-making powers in the churches, and the persons taking the powers were usually those men who had money. This pattern has not changed much since Reformation times.

Thus the churches recognize wealth, and seem to have no problem with there being no limit on how much money a person makes. If it is okay for men to have unlimited income, the same should apply to women. Yet it seems that the first question asked of a woman working is whether or not she needs the money. Or, a female graduate student isn't considered for an assistantship if the professors don't think she "needs" the money. That question doesn't arise for the male students.

Much as the issue of needing money shouldn't be applied unfairly to women, it is an important and valid question within one's own value structure and life decision-making. Is money to be earned just because you need it? Or is money in some way an end in itself? It would seem that overall in our society money is an end in itself—the more we have, the more we think we need, and the more ready we are to justify whatever we do in order to get more money.

One result of the present unemployment is that the realities surrounding money are imposing themselves on us more and more. We are being forced to choose between what is necessary and what is not; and we are amazed at what is not necessary. We are beginning to choose what is important to us and what is not. When there is money, we spend it, sometimes on anything that an advertiser makes sound good. And when we can keep making more and more money, we go after it, no matter the cost to our own selves and to our families. Unemployment has stopped that process.

Women raising a family alone usually know very well the value of money, and what is necessary and what is not. Women are still so close to the poverty line, if not still in poverty, that they have little experience having flexibility in using money.

Money for basic needs—housing, food, clothing—is necessary unless we want to chance becoming wards of the government. That doesn't seem like a viable option, and hardly fair to others who are trying to care for themselves and be responsible in their commitments and life decisions. So let us take this amount of money as a given. Beyond that, though, is the freedom to choose between making more money and using the time and energy for other things. Our vocational focus does not *have* to be trained on money, except to meet basic needs.

Taking this step in our society means stepping away from what might be considered a normal value system and life-style.

PERSONAL VALUES

Most of us find out what is important to us by loss, or through obtaining something we thought we wanted and/ or needed and finding it unsatisfying. Many times we do have to go through that process, which in itself is satisfying, though often painful.

Sorting out our personal values is perhaps the most important step in making life decisions, small and large. We all tend to learn these values through our mistakes. We are forced to deal with such issues as:

Is it more important to pretend to love someone to save a marriage than to get a divorce?

Is it more important to play the role of devoted mother than to try to mix career and marriage/ family when the latter produces conflict in the home but makes us happier?

Should we be honest with ourselves, or is it better to keep busy and play the roles we have taken on ourselves?

Do we want an honest relationship with a man or husband more than no relationship at all?

Is it more important to have status and money than to be happy and satisfied with what we are doing? how we are living?

For centuries people have been able to ignore these questions just by not having the freedom to move in and out of jobs, of marriage and relationships, of commitments. We have a free society that fosters independence and development of the individual. Christianity stresses the relationship of the individual to God, the growth of the individual, though as a member of God's family. In the United States we value the person doing something on her or his own—pulling oneself up by the bootstraps; meeting the challenge of the unknown; building a business with one's own guts, ingenuity, and even manipulation and use of others.

So, no matter how committed we are to the group, we have in us a rather extreme individuality, which will not be denied. As a result our value decisions must take into account our own personhood, not just what we want to be doing with and for others as a member of a family or community.

The women's movement has heightened the declaration of independence of women in this society. This was necessitated by the already existent independence of men, often at the expense of women. To be equal, therefore, is also to be independent. There is little within this society to help us turn more toward each other, sharing, giving, caring within our communities, within our nation, and among nations. And, though we may want to work toward this end, we must also recognize that the society presently demands a person be an individual in her or his own right, *or* be subjected to another. There is not a communal commitment nor structure, not even in the churches. This communal commitment may well be a personal value that many of us have but have not been able to pursue very directly through existing organizational structures.

The churches, men and women in the churches, may well be the ones to find the needed structures to make it possible for us to be together, to know the oneness of God and God's family, to give without being treated as though we are nonpersons. Personally, this value is more important than all others, so the definition of and need for money falls into a more general category of survival. But this doesn't mean at all that I have found the way to reach my goal. What I have found is what doesn't take me there—not the women's movement, not political organizations, not jobs in which the end product was to help people. The closest I seem to have been able to come is through playing string quartets with the same people over a period of time and through playing for and with a church choir. Perhaps music, another language, makes it possible for all those involved to express themselves and to give in ways we cannot through words.

I have also found some of this communication among waitresses. A bond has developed among some of the waitresses with whom I work that gives us the strength to make it through tense situations and work crises hardly touched by the pressure. Much of the time we have an effective support network of giving and caring about each other. We look forward to seeing each other. Interestingly enough, we are there and working to make money, but most of us are at the survival point so there is no competition based on what anyone has or doesn't have. We know each of us has to earn enough to pay a mortgage or rent, to buy food, to pay utility bills, to buy gas for the car.

We each have to work out our own personal values. I found the work conditions for positions in which I made what I thought was a lot of money were destroying me— my self-worth, my self-confidence, my love for others, my need to give of myself to others. Now I try to do only the things that allow me to be me at the same time that I work to survive and pursue my life goals and personal values.

Work situations confront a person with some very basic issues. For example, is it important to be honest with others and with yourself? Some employers cannot tolerate such a level of honesty, nor the demand for it which a worker may place on the employer simply by wanting to be honest. Is it important to love yourself and others?

Can you and/or will you play the power games so often required in the workplace? Is it important to you to know that what you are doing in the workplace is not harmful to others? There are many levels of hurt to others, from producing weapons and devices for chemical warfare to creating environmental pollution to damaging a fellow employee through poor personnel practices.

If we are to be true to God, and to ourselves, we have to find ways to live and work according to our values. Identifying those values comes first, and even that may be a lifelong process. Yet every vocational decision must involve a careful analysis of the impact and reflection of our values.

MONEY MANAGEMENT AND COMMITMENTS

Whether or not we aim to obtain sizable amounts of money is a value question. Having and managing money is also essential to survival. The way your money is managed directly affects your independence, your work, your life-style.

The American way is to finish high school, go to college or postsecondary school, get a job, get married, buy a home, and have children. Can you afford it? It seems as though with each passing day each of these steps becomes more and more costly.

The first step in money management is to prepare a budget. To do this, you list your income, and you list your expenditures. Don't forget payments such as insurance that come up once a year. And don't forget local wage taxes as well as state and federal taxes. Build in some extra in expenditures for increases in gasoline costs, in heating, electricity, and telephone bills, and for home and car maintenance and repair. How comprehensive is your health insurance, and are you paying for it, or is your employer? Build in any costs you may have, including the deductible for an emergency. We never know what may happen.

Your budget for expenditures must have leeway to allow for the unexpected, unplanned cost. Your budget will tell you whether or not you can afford to drive to work; whether or not you can eat out for lunch regularly; whether or not drinks after work are financially feasible; whether or not to join a health club or spa; whether or not to take some courses.

It is wise to plan to save a regular amount of money each week, or each month, to be put into a savings or a retirement account. This money can be planned, too, perhaps just for long-range financial security; a fallback in case of an emergency; a child's education; the down payment for a home.

In planning savings and investment pay particular attention to tax laws. There is not a lot of benefit in saving money and then paying income tax on the interest, which just might throw you into a higher income tax bracket and you end up losing money. Several financial counselors emphasize that the best way to increase your savings is to plan to reduce your taxes, and then to recoup that money at a later time. The Individual Retirement Account (IRA) now available lets you save money and not pay income tax on the amount saved up to a certain amount until you take the money out of the account, at which time your income will probably be lower and you in a lower tax bracket.

The main financial incentive to owning your own home is the ability to deduct the interest in the mortgage payment on your federal income tax. When you consider that nearly all of the mortgage payment in the first few years is interest (plus insurance and property taxes), not principal, you realize this is a sizable deduction. Property taxes are also deductible. If you are renting, you are helping someone else make mortgage payments and allowing them the benefits of the tax deductions. It is possible you would save money by paying a mortgage a good deal higher than what rent would cost, just through tax deductions and reimbursement.

Buying a home is not so easy today as it was a few years ago. Banks are asking down payments of 20 percent of the cost of the home, and the total mortgage payment usually cannot exceed 25 percent of one's income. Interest rates skyrocketed a couple of years ago, which put home buying out of reach for most of us. The rates dropped considerably in late 1982.

People are losing their homes and their cars these days because they cannot meet payment schedules. This today is not because they have not been able to plan their finances, but because their income was radically reduced through unemployment. We have come to expect job security and to depend on income security when making long-term financial commitments such as taking out a mortgage. The present state of the economy is causing most of us to be less secure, and a lot more careful about purchases which we don't have the money in hand to buy.

Money management should be a means to obtaining some freedom from continuing financial worries and stress. When you know how much you have, how much you can anticipate, then you know how much you have to spend. Spending beyond this will produce problems, stress, anxieties, and pressures no one needs. When you manage your money, you can consider a job change, or a reduction in benefits or salary, or a special purchase, because you can plan it out financially. Money management and planning is integral to any life-planning or decision-making.

How we spend our money reflects our values. We need to look closely at what we use our money for. We can learn a lot about ourselves, our priorities, our direction. If the way we spend our money does not reflect what we think are our life goals, then we need to reexamine both the goals and our spending and make adjustments accordingly.

When there are several members in a family, and everyone is not attuned to budgeting and financial management, serious financial and family problems can develop. It doesn't take much to throw a budget off. Christmas gift buying can do it. Or just buying more expensive meats regularly. Or entertaining one extra time a month. Or turning the heat up during an extra cold spell. Or leaving the lights on all night. Children can begin to learn money management very young. And it is important to the family that every member understand the concept of management, so that they are not as likely as otherwise constantly to be making money demands. Advertisers play on the readiness of children to want this or that, and to pester their parents.

Some women make money demands on their spouse. When other elements are lacking in the marriage, the wife seems to zero in on making the man buy things for her. In some ways this makes the marriage more manageable for the husband, too, since he is expected to bring home money, and he can understand that demand.

MONEY AND MATERIAL VALUES

A woman, a man, or a family who adopts the material values of the society will have certain aspirations for possessions and for ongoing financial expenditures. These often include:

> owning their own home
> owning one or more cars, perhaps newer models
> furnishing the home with suites
> belonging to certain membership clubs

> going to the beauty salon regularly
> entertaining regularly
> dressing in fashion
> buying the children the latest fad in games, clothing,
>   equipment
> playing golf or tennis
> having a full complement of household appliances,
>   stereo, special lighting

Put together, this life-style, especially if it includes private schools for the children, can be expensive. The individual or family needs to consider what it can realistically afford, and not go beyond that. If having these things is considered necessary to the family, then plans have to be made to bring in enough income to purchase all the goods and services. Such money requirements set limits to the flexibility of the woman or the man in determining what job to have, or even how many jobs. Value judgments are made here as to whether it is more important for the parents to be at home, or to be out working to have additional money. Sometimes the parent has the job that allows the time to be at home and also pays enough to make it possible to purchase all the material things the family thinks it needs to "belong."

The pressures from trying to keep "up with the Joneses" have forced any number of individuals and families to withdraw from the whole scene. They decide to go off on their own and be themselves. Some have bought farms in Vermont and are becoming self-sufficient. Their work is now at home, and it is family work, in the agricultural sense of life-styles over centuries. Obviously we cannot all go back to the farm, nor would it be right for us. The options for working but still being true to ourselves are there around us. Farming is one.

Others have dropped out of the work world and gone on welfare. Although this is an option, it is difficult to see how it is a long-term resolution to an individual's desire to do God's will and to seek lifelong goals. Still this seems to be a necessary step for some people in breaking the cycle of wanting material things and pushing themselves to do anything to make money. The thousands of people finding themselves suddenly unemployed have been faced with a cut in their material goods. Many have tried to continue their same life-style and now are faced with terrible debts, threat of having utilities turned off, and all the rest. They still *believe* they will be called back to work, even when their unemployment benefits run out.

Underneath the economic turmoil and lack of jobs this country is now experiencing is a crisis in values. The time is right for us to take a good look at our values and our life goals and to direct ourselves consciously toward them, while ensuring the means to survive.

Many people are back to the "cottage" industry, just as others have gone "back" to the farm. They produce goods and services in their homes and sell them to friends, neighbors, community stores. A countereconomy of individuals selling their skills and trades is developing, separate from the more formal work force of the large employers. Record-keeping, reporting, bookkeeping are at a minimum. People make the arrangements with each other in their own communities, and it seems to be working. Those who need help are obtaining it, and those who need to "work" are "working."

To most of us these people are not working, but by any reasonable definition of work, they are. They have left what we have come to know as the workplace. They no longer have to get up each morning and catch a bus or drive through rush-hour traffic. They have more freedom and more options in their lives. They may actually work longer hours, but the work takes on a different role in their lives.

Women have always been part of this countereconomy which is now growing so rapidly. Women sew for others, bake for others, do handiwork that they sell, baby-sit, clean. How many older women do you know that have made a living this way for years, perhaps even raised a family on such an income? Any number of women have run farms by themselves. Although we have come to see women as having been excluded from the world of work, women have survived, even thrived. Being part of the countereconomy, where women have thought themselves to fail, may turn out to be one of the most effective means to survive, as a whole person as well as financially.

Money does buy material goods, and it is the means to survival. We need money. But we also need to nurture the whole self. Our value system should reflect the place that money holds for us. This in turn will determine much of our decision-making about vocation and life goals.

SOME QUESTIONS TO CONSIDER

VALUES: WHAT IS MOST IMPORTANT?

Is it money, and what can be bought with that money?

Is it having a healthy and happy family, husband and children, with or without the money to buy a nice home, clothing, private schooling?

Is it having close friends and time to spend with those friends?

Is it having a job that is challenging and satisfying, and perhaps the central point in your life?

Is it having power and influence over others, whether at work, in the home, or in the community?

Is it maintaining yourself independently and having the freedom to make changes dependent on needs and interests?

Is it maintaining yourself independently and having the freedom to read, think, be creative as you want and need?

Is it having a family and being creative through the family structure?

Is it having the emotional satisfaction of husband, with or without family?

Is it developing your potential as a person, perhaps in a number of directions?

Is it developing your career potential?

Is it serving other people?

WHAT IS MY FINANCIAL STATUS?

Every individual or family needs a basic budget to determine how much income is required and what money may be available for extra expenditures.

Living Costs	*Cost/Month*	*Cost/Year*
Housing		
Mortgage or Rent		
Utilities		
heat		
electricity		
telephone		
water		
sewerage		
Insurance		
Upkeep/Maintenance		
Repairs		
Food		
Clothing		

Transportation
  Car
  Gasoline
  Tires
  Maintenance
  Repair
  Insurance
  Public Transportation
Health Care
  Insurance
  Eye/Ear Care
  Doctor Visits
  Dentist Visits
  Prescriptions
  Deductibles
Hobbies
Leisure/Recreation Activities
Vacation
Child Care
Household Supplies (nonfood)
Pet Care and Food
Taxes
  Property (if not included in mortgage)
  Federal and State Income
  Local
Miscellaneous

Income	*Month*	*Year*

List the income of each income-
  producing member
  of the family *by* the source
Interest and Dividends
Rent from property
Other (List)

CHAPTER 7

Decision-Making—
Setting Life Goals

We have looked at the world of work, at the family and interpersonal relationships, and at money. Now we need to mesh the opportunities and problems and needs and challenges to produce the decisions necessary for the fulfillment of our vocation.

At the end of some chapters you had questions to think and work through. This should have helped you to start making your decisions. Following are summary questions that will start you on your way to developing your life plan. All the questions need to be used in a creative, open, manner. Even the answers need to be somewhat open, for a plan must be alive, must be constantly changing, while at the same time providing direction.

1. My Vocation (Describe your life goals in general terms).
2. What is the role of other people in my reaching my life goals, my following my vocation?
    spouse or partner
    friends
    children
    other family
    teachers

minister
other people (i.e., people in need)
3. How do I spend my time, and how do these activities fit into my vocation?

Activity   *Time*   *Purpose*   *Goal*

4. What are my material and financial wants and needs?
5. What skills do I want or need to develop?
6. What responsibilities do I have within my
    family
    church
    home
    community
7. What is most important to me now?

From your answers to the above questions and those to the questions at the ends of chapters begin to write your life plan. Prepare some immediate and long-range goals addressing at least the following:
    education, training, skill development
    work
    family/children
    money
    material belongings
    service in community, church
    personal development (prayer, reading, medita-
        tion alone or with others; exercise; health care)
    personal behavior (some specifics to help you
        reflect your values and goals)

Does your plan reflect your values and priorities? Test it. Will it help you fulfill your vocation?

You might also try to think back a few years and write out what you think your life plan was then, though not formalized. Have you changed? Are you heading in the same direction? Your priorities probably have changed, but your values may well be the same. Do you consider these values in all your decision-making? This process can again help us to know ourselves better. As any historian would tell us, we must know our past before we can know our present, or try to plan our future.

DEVELOPING LIFE PATTERNS

We all know people struggling to make their lives come together. Some may call it vocation; others are just trying to develop a life pattern that works for them. The following are a few vignettes on some women, and men, whom I know.

A is twenty-eight years old, single—divorced, without children. She is well educated, bright, well read, but resists holding a job in the regular world of work because she wants to make a living as a violinist. She also wants a relationship that is positive for her being; to date she has found herself in relationships that seemed to negate her existence. Through a sort of withdrawing she has developed a life-style that is comfortable and productive for her. She spends time with friends; reads; practices and studies. She plays as many jobs as she can get.

B is an attractive woman in her late twenties who is successful in the world of work. She directs a major government agency and earns a good salary. She is spoken of frequently as a political candidate potential. She is married to an attorney who has a successful practice. Two years ago they decided to begin their family. Both have continued full-time in their careers and jobs. They have the money to purchase the help and services to keep the home running smoothly, leaving time to be spent with the baby.

C is an only child who wanted a large family. She and her husband now have six wonderful, loving children.

She works full-time keeping the home and the children functioning, and tries to sew on the side for additional income. Every member of the family is active in the church, in the school, in the community, and they all seem to have so much to give. C has channeled all her energies into her family and volunteer work, and brings much love and pleasure to those around her

D is a single parent with a daughter, twenty, now living away from home. Mother and daughter grew together in developing an independent and self-sufficient life-style. The daughter felt a lot of pressure for material goods from her peers in school, but is now beginning to understand better what material things are and are not for her. Both pursue their personal values, quite free from the patterns of those around, which has made them rather separate. Both enjoy being with people, but also treasure time alone. Both find it difficult to meet the requirements imposed on the person by the traditional work and social situations. Both are seeking alternatives that will allow them to live and at the same time to fulfill their life goals, their vocations. In many ways the mother and the daughter are each still actively seeking their vocation.

E is age twenty-eight and has been married for three years. She and her husband have no children, but want to. E has a good job, but is not fulfilled by her work and feels many pressures from her work situation which violate her values. She is artistic and enjoys keeping a home, sewing, cooking, gardening. Her husband is a skilled tradesperson and very supportive of her personal and career development. They both give extensively of themselves to other family members, and to their community. E is volunteering time and money to get a newspaper started, her dream, and has full support from her husband. She is still seeking ways to utilize her talents and skills and fulfill herself.

F is a middle-aged woman who took on the responsibility of raising four children when her husband left years ago. She never remarried. All the children are now grown and F is raising two of the grandchildren. She is strong, capable, and committed to improving the lives of people. She works very hard as director of a social service agency, and has developed over the years excellent administrative skills. She has a male supervisor who respects and listens to her, and supports her in her work and her goals. When they disagree on something, they can communicate this and talk it through. She is able to make it work. She has put together family, work, and community while at the same time growing as a person and fulfilling her life goals.

As we seek our vocations we need to keep in mind that other women are seeking theirs, too. We need each other. We need to help and support each other, no matter what one or the other is doing.

If my lifework is to have a night job cleaning rest rooms and offices, I want and need you to respect me and my work. I want you to appreciate what I do. If my work is guarding people in prison, I want and need you to respect me and my work. If my work is being a business executive, I want you to respect me and my work.

We need to share our work and our love. We must come to know in our hearts that no one of us is better than another. We all need each other, and we all are seeking to love and to be loved as God would have us.

Alone, we fail. Together, working and sharing and supporting each other, we shall succeed, as God may will.